Shared Parenting

Raising your children cooperatively after separation

Jill Burrett & Michael Green

FINCH PUBLISHING
SYDNEY

Advance praise for this book

'Separation and divorce can be an extremely difficult time not only for parents themselves but also for children, who can feel frightened and confused. Whatever the circumstances of separation and divorce, we know that children – no matter what age – want to stay connected with both of their parents. The authors of *Shared Parenting* share both their professional and personal experiences and knowledge in the area of parenting and families. Their practical style of writing gives parents real situations to think about and the practical tools to find ways to *really* share the parenting and to continue meaningful relationships with their children after the break-up.

'This is a must-read for any parent contemplating separation and divorce or for those already in the process. It's never too late to reconnect with your children. The short- and long-term benefits for parents and children far outway any immediate difficulties. You and your kids deserve this.'

Judy Radich
National President
Early Childhood Australia

'Research all over the world has shown that it is best for children to have both parents actively involved in their lives despite the parents' separation, except where there is child abuse, ongoing violence or intractable conflict. This book is an excellent resource for people who want to understand how best to put the children first and to work out cooperative, shared parenting arrangements after separation. It is full of useful information, practical wisdom and sensible advice. I recommend it very highly.'

Patrick Parkinson
Professor of Law
University of Sydney

'This book should be compulsory reading for all separating parents. We know children cope best with a family break-up when their parents work together to share their care. But it isn't easy. Burrett and Green have the experience and knowledge to provide practical advice that gives parents a very valuable blueprint for making it happen.'

Bettina Arndt
Social commentator

'Negotiating parenting time following separation is complex and emotional, and often a source of ongoing conflict. This book offers practical solutions focussed on children's needs, while challenging some traditional assumptions about parenting after separation.'

Anne Hollonds
CEO, Relationships Australia (NSW)

'*Shared Parenting* is a blueprint for divorcing parents to use as they try to figure out the next steps of being parents. The book is full of helpful hints, probing questions and answers, and is a highly readable and engaging tool for parents to use. It serves as a tremendously useful guide to rebuilding relationships post-divorce. Any parent going through a divorce can learn from it.

'*Shared Parenting* challenges divorcing parents to focus on their children's interest above their own. It is a superb resource to help parents define their post-divorce relationship in a way that is best for their family needs and in a way that most clearly meets the needs of their children. The book offers insights and practical solutions to the complex issues and questions that arise during the break-up of any family.

'*Shared Parenting* encourages mothers and fathers to refocus their attention away from the negatives of divorce towards the positives of co-parenting, with the clear focus on the best interests of the children. This book is highly useful in asking and answering the questions all parents must consider as they develop a new family plan and dynamic to ensure that the children do not lose either parent and that their children's needs are paramount.'

Jody Mosten, Ph.D.
Clinical psychologist
Los Angeles

Shared Parenting: Raising your children cooperatively after separation
This edition first published in 2006 in Australia and New Zealand by Finch
Publishing Pty Limited, PO Box 120, Lane Cove, NSW 1595, Australia. ABN 49
057 285 248

10 09 08 07 06   8 7 6 5 4 3 2

National Library of Australia Cataloguing-in-Publication entry

Burrett, Jill F.
Shared parenting: raising your children cooperatively
after separation

Bibliography.
ISBN 1 876451 72 6.

1. Parenting, Part-time. 2. Children of single parents. 3.
Children of divorced parents. I. Green, Michael, 1939- .
II. Title.
649.10243

Edited by Sean Doyle
Editorial assistance from Rosemary Peers
Text designed and typeset in Galliard 11/15pt by J&M Typesetting
Cover design by Steve Miller – 154 Design
Cover photograph courtesy of Jupiter Images
Printed by Southwood Press

Notes The 'Authors' notes' section at the back of this book contains useful
additional information and references to quoted material in the text. Each reference
is linked to the text by its relevant page number and an identifying line entry.

Disclaimers While every care has been taken in researching and compiling the
information in this book, it is in no way intended to replace professional legal
advice and counselling. Readers are encouraged to seek such help as they deem
necessary. The authors and publisher specifically disclaim any liability arising from
the application of information in this book.

Other Finch titles can be viewed at **www.finch.com.au**

Contents

Introduction

• • • • • • • • • • • • • • • • • • • •

Equal shared parenting is the new way to look at parenting after separation and divorce. In many countries (including the United Kingdom, the United States, New Zealand, Canada and Australia) cooperative shared parenting has for decades been rightly regarded as the best way of ensuring children of divorced parents adjust well to family change, so in many ways it's actually nothing new. But because for so long it's been presumed that dads either can't or don't want to be involved more often than fortnightly (and even that they aren't sufficiently competent to do more!), equal shared parenting seems new, challenging the assumption that upon separation children live with one parent *or* the other. For far too long there's been a misplaced belief that children, especially those under 10, are better off with mothers – and this has helped to spawn another (hotly debated) belief: that the legal system disadvantages fathers.

We believe that this situation has seriously disadvantaged children, and that fathers should be more engaged with their children than they have been. This requires real time, just like most mothers have always known – and given. We also believe that, for a very long time, gender stereotypes, 'the system' and other complex prejudices have discouraged some fathers and caused others to participate little in parenting, especially after separating.

We don't think fortnightly weekend parenting is meaningful shared parenting. We think that *shared parenting means having real chunks of time engaged with your children for a flexible 35–50 percent or more of their available time.* Official inquiries into separated parenting are currently being conducted in many countries, in particular into whether there should be a presumption that equal shared parenting be the norm. Mostly, these inquiries have been unable to endorse a general policy that can help families when every family is different and when some, sadly, are seriously dysfunctional. Families who use welfare services and courts, and cannot arrive at satisfactory solutions through mediation and counselling services, are very likely to be families where shared parenting isn't going to work for the children. A general presumption of equal shared parenting therefore has some hazards and is unlikely to become official policy or law. However, its serious contemplation as a basic presumption is a good start towards de-marginalising fathers, who need and deserve encouragement.

Fathers' protest groups (such as *Fathers4Justice* in the UK, *Papa Separati* in Italy and *SOS Papa* in Spain) have sometimes found themselves forced to take extreme measures in order to get attention in policy-making circles, and have sometimes risked disrepute to get their views heard. For instance, one member of *Fathers4Justice*, dressed in a Batman suit, perched himself on a ledge of Buckingham Palace. Batman suits were also worn by several protesters outside the Colosseum in Rome. In Madrid, two men – protected by fireproof suits – doused themselves in petrol and set fire to themselves outside the Spanish Parliament.

A serious rethink of contemporary parenting policy and practice is not before time. *Sole-mother 'custody', with mother doing all the parenting and father merely paying the bills and popping into the kids' lives from time to time, isn't really good enough for children – and often not for mothers – in either separated or 'intact' family situations.*

We want to:

■ help co-parents get real about what's possible for their own families, in their own unique circumstances. Gearing your life around children's real needs demands great self-sacrifice and compromise. If you aren't really up to full-on shared parenting, maybe you shouldn't be signing up for it. If you are, we want to encourage you to do it well.

■ help you to be self-responsible and creative about separated parenting. We recognise that for many mothers shared parenting is difficult to contemplate, and for many fathers it's difficult to achieve.

■ discourage you from following misplaced advice from the wrong people, and help you get reliably informed about the myths and realities of child psychology and legal precedents.

■ help you avoid using the legal system except for its mediation and information services.

About this book

We've called this book *Shared Parenting* so that it's obvious we're talking about co-parenting with equal or close-to-equal amounts of time with your children. However, we do want to discourage parents from *competing* over percentages of hours, days or nights. *How much time the children spend with each of their parents must be about what's going to work well for them, not about what's fair for you.*

We make many references to parent education and parenting programs, but detailed coverage of these is beyond the scope of this book. Many good courses and self-help books are available (see the 'Helpful resources' section at the back of this book). We confine our discussion of parenting after divorce to time-sharing specifically.

We have divided up our text into what seems to us logical sections, wanting to keep it an easy read. We base what we have to say on our own research and on our experience of what works and what doesn't for real people who have consulted us professionally over the years. We've also drawn on child development theory and the results of reliable research reports, mainly from Australia, the UK and the US. New research is happening all the time, stimulated in particular by increasing recognition among policy-makers of the importance of active, engaged parenting. In order to encourage you to explore further the research we rely on, we have referenced this in the 'Authors' notes' at the back of the book.

We believe that research on patterns of parenting after separation has not so far been able to reliably demonstrate a preferred way of dividing parenting time for all families after separation. However, our research and experience shows that what certainly predicts a good outcome for your kids is competent parenting that is genuinely child-focused, however you divide up the time slots, provided you both have plenty of time with them.

Jill Burrett and Michael Green

Personal reflections

● ● ● ● ● ● ● ● ● ● ● ● ● ● ● ● ● ● ● ●

Jill

I first had the idea of another separated parenting book because in my consulting practice there seemed to be new kinds of issues presenting themselves for people facing up to separation. I recognise that many parents don't seek the advice and counsel of psychologists because they make their own private arrangements, so my clients aren't necessarily representative across the board. But because of the high profile that shared parenting has been getting lately, I am being approached by some parents who are very troubled at the prospect of sharing their children, as well as by parents who are keen to share the care of even very young children equally.

Although I have survived a divorce (albeit after a childless partnership) and have been a keen stepmother for twenty-four years as a consequence of my second marriage, I have not had direct experience of shared parenting except through my clients. However, I do know personally about how your feelings can run riot when you're hurt and disappointed because your partner lets you down – distorting your judgement for a long time – and how a person you really loved and committed to can turn from a soulmate into someone from a different planet, impossible to see eye-to-eye with. I also know personally about a long-distance 'shared' parenting arrangement that somehow survived the years of geographical separation because of goodwill, tolerance, acceptance and a positive outlook. These attitudes are important, in fact essential for shared parenting. And I do know first-hand about the very strong bonds that can develop between half-siblings despite their different upbringings.

As a mother myself, as well as a child development 'expert', I am gravely concerned at the idea of a newborn baby spending seven days with one parent and seven days with another. My concern extends to the not-so-newborn, who – quite naturally – has to make the transition through the months from infancy to toddlerdom, and who will not thrive if their attachments to important caregivers are regularly interrupted for significant lengths of time (i.e. days at a stretch). I'm also concerned about parents being so protective of their children that they unwittingly discourage the development of emotional independence by limiting time with their other parent for the wrong reasons. However, I have always felt that fathers ought to be more involved with their children than they seem to feel they're expected to be, or than their ex-partners sometimes 'allow' them to be. I believe that if parenting responsibilities were shared more equally in *all* families, children would not only be better off, but there would not be so many difficulties sharing children after a separation. Something radical needs to be done to encourage fathers to share effectively – and to help mothers share at all.

How is more equally-shared parenting after separation going to work? How can it truly benefit children, given that it isn't what most parents have in mind when they commit to partnership and parenthood? And given that many parents seem to get caught up in notions of entitlement and fairness that don't have much to do with their children's emotional needs? A new look at separated parenting was obviously needed, and writing with an experienced father (my co-author, Michael) was absolutely what was required! I wanted to challenge old assumptions and to help fathers and mothers enhance their parenting and 'get real' about their motives and attitudes, so they have the best chance of 'getting it right'. So I took another hard look at what was and wasn't working, and what the new research is showing – that is what has guided our advice and ideas as this book has come into being.

May 2006

Michael

Why is it that so many separated men and women are unable to sort out sensible parenting arrangements without a massive amount of anger, bitterness and trauma – to say nothing of the accompanying waste of time, money and energy?

The key mistake made by many couples is not to accept that their world has changed. After separation and divorce, the world is changed for mother, father and children. It is not the same world any more. The family is a different family, a father is a different father, a mother is a different mother. The relationships between children and parents are irrevocably changed, no matter where or with whom they live. So everyone has to change, too.

Failure to acknowledge this can lead to a mother striving to establish a home situation that is unchanged in all aspects except one: the father is no longer there. Or it can lead to a father seeing himself in the same role as before, i.e. the provider who leaves it to the mother to do the nurturing, and who himself now pops into the children's lives once a fortnight or so. It results in the children having one home base, one close parental relationship and one distant one.

Not many separated parents are happy with this. Women, wanting to reestablish themselves in society and work, find the burden of parenting alone overwhelming. Men find that they have so little meaningful time with their children that they are reduced to onlookers in their lives. And all the research points to children being very unhappy with this outcome and wanting something quite different.

What they want is a true relationship with both parents, and real time to foster it. This is what shared parenting is about.

What is shared parenting? It is an arrangement following separation whereby children have two homes and spend substantial amounts of time – including weekends and weekdays – with parents who share in their upbringing and development. In practice it means:

- children spending ordinary and fun times with each parent
- children sleeping, eating, working and playing in each home
- each parent listening and talking to the children
- the parents sharing the big decisions about the children's lives
- each parent being involved in the children's schools, sport, music and other activities
- each parent being fully aware of the physical, intellectual and emotional health of the children, and

- children being part of two extended families – grandparents, uncles and aunts, cousins, friends.

My views are based on over ten years' experience with separated couples, in the courts, in mediation, in group work and in individual counselling, as well as on my own personal experience as a separated father. I have done a lot of reading and research in this area of human behaviour. Opinions and conclusions differ and can be subjective and untested, but I think there are some common themes.

In preparing material for this book, I spoke to many separated mothers and fathers who were 'doing' shared parenting. Their responses – some of which are included in the following text – were remarkably similar. *It was tough at first, but it worked because they:*

- recognised that their world had changed
- accepted that they – mother, father and children – had to change
- put to one side their anger, bitterness and emotion
- put their children's welfare before their own comfort
- communicated, got help, and learnt
- acknowledged that their children wanted both parents, and
- stuck at it.

May 2006

1 Parenting after separation

● ● ● ● ● ● ● ● ● ● ● ● ● ● ●

Separation always disrupts the familiar patterns of family life. Routines and responsibilities that have established themselves as the family grew and developed have to be renegotiated. How your family operated probably came about without a lot of proactive planning. It's unlikely that either of you parents worried too much, especially in happier times, about who did what, how much actual time you each spent doing the hands-on stuff of day-to-day family life, even though sometimes one of you might have felt unfairly overloaded or unsupported!

'It was the biggest emotional upheaval of my life. There are so many clichés about break-ups being bad, damaging and bitter, although ours wasn't. It was just the sheer sadness and disappointment that things

didn't work out how we'd planned, which at times
I found overwhelming, that was the hardest part to
deal with while trying to be positive about the future
for the kids.' NAOMI

Why families work well

Even though today's break-up rates seem to seriously suggest that something about committed partnerships isn't
working, traditional family life does work for children, if not
always for parents. It has its own in-built efficiencies, which
are useful, whatever might be happening between Mum and
Dad that isn't too good. Children can see both of the most
important people in their lives (you two!) every day. Busy
parents can feel in touch and connected with everyone on
very little time. One parent covers the lion's share of the
domestic minutiae of lunch boxes and spelling lists, and gets
increasingly efficient at it. The other spends more time away
from home at work (and becomes increasingly efficient at
it), swinging in at weekends with more family stuff. Each
parent takes on areas of responsibility that fit their skills,
availability and interests, and a natural division with common-
sense delegation of domestic activities develops. Your adult
partnership needs are met at home with your children's natural parent. Whatever partnership frustrations and disap-
pointments you are struggling with, the family you have
created is the only one your children know, and is what they
depend on totally for their security. It's an effective and
uncomplicated arrangement for your kids that meets their
growing needs even if it doesn't always work for you!

Why separating means facing big changes

Two different homes because you're living separately has to mean that all this changes. There's no overlapping. When you're 'on duty' you have to be able to meet *all* the kids' needs, and at the same time find a way to have a life for yourself outside of the parenting arena. You have to adjust to a 'full-on' or 'full-off' kind of 'shiftwork' parenting. You may have to go for days without seeing your kids, and you mightn't have bargained on making that adjustment till they were much older. You might have blended your working life during the week with brief family interaction, mornings and evenings, with the real fun stuff at the weekends and on family holidays. But separation puts an end to this. You might have expected your hands-on weekday routine to last for years to come, to have mapped out your future for you. Now the kids are off to their other home for parts of the week, leaving you feeling stranded and unsettled.

> *'At the beginning, I really missed my son when he went to his father's home. It was week-about and later fortnight-about. I felt cheated of my motherhood, restless and unsettled when he wasn't around me. I cried a lot. But gradually it all fell into place.'* JANE

Staying in a relationship that isn't working because you're dreading being an out-of-touch, occasional parent is about as unsatisfactory as staying in one because you're afraid of separating and having to share your children with their other parent for long periods of time. Both of these apprehensions are quite natural. By and large, mums still do most of the hands-on parenting and presume that they are going to continue this after separation. So they often resist shared parenting. On the other hand, dads who have assumed a breadwinning role may not have done much hands-on stuff, and they rightly fear having to suffer an occasional parenting role after separating. However, given the opportunity, they may be prepared to make lifestyle changes to progress to fuller parenting responsibilities.

The scene is set for you both to start worrying about what's fair, what's right, how to juggle everything so you don't lose touch, whether the kids will love you less if you're not there all the time, who's going to pay for everything to do with the kids, how a parent who's never been around much for them can look after them properly, etc. A minefield of potential grievances and uncertainties!

Research on the outcomes for children of divorce has produced varied results. However, there is agreement that separation can bring serious risks for children in a number of ways. Currently, about 80 percent of children of separated families live in sole-mother custody arrangements, and as many as a third of them have little or no contact with their fathers. The common arrangement for parenting children after divorce – living with Mum and visiting Dad – often leaves everyone dissatisfied. There is evidence that it does little for solid parent–child relationships, and can reduce one parent to onlooker status. Children cared for mainly by mothers can too easily lose contact with their fathers. Mothers can find parenting on their own a tough task, and need relief and support. Fathers who experience difficulties in contact often

withdraw from their children's lives, with negative consequences for themselves and for the children.

But recent research brings us good news: children in
shared-care arrangements are more satisfied and appear to
be better adjusted on several levels; and many studies show
that most parents with majority care want their ex-partners
to see more of the children.

Your children will not suffer long term because you separated if they have time with both of you – and if you both
support this arrangement amicably and flexibly. They *will*
suffer if you only think about what's fair for *you*, and if you
criticise or interfere with each other's parenting.

*'Shared parenting gives both parents the opportunity
to be real parents. The kids develop a strong
relationship with both of you. You don't have the
burden that single parents have, and you avoid the
desolation of being a "non-parent".'* JIM

What should parents do?

As yet there is no scientific evidence to back a preferred way
of dividing parenting time after separating. Because families
are all so different, no one post-divorce arrangement can
be said to be in the best interests of all children. What is
certain, though, is that *what predicts a good outcome for your
kids is competent parenting,* however you divide up the time
slots. It's *how* you parent, not how many hours you put in,
that matters, although quantity of time is relevant because it
supports quality parenting.

We tend to approach parenting as if it's a talent that just comes *because* we became parents. But it takes insight, patience, self-sacrifice and regular self-analysis, especially in today's challenging times. Separation is a great opportunity to rethink your parenting priorities. Your children need time with both of their parents, time that is meaningful. They need to feel you are available to them, giving them guidance, sympathy, discipline, comfort, supervision, and conveying a strong sense of their importance to you despite your other priorities and interests. Quality parenting takes time, but having time with your children is no guarantee *in itself* that your parenting is going to be meaningful and constructive, unless you make sure it is. What your kids want, need and deserve is emotional commitment and active participation from both of you, however their time with you is divided, provided you *both* have plenty of time with them.

Shared parenting can produce happier children and more satisfied parents

Q: Is it normal for a child to spend the weekends regularly away from friends and belongings, especially if that parent (usually Dad) wants to absorb his child into the household as if they were there all the time?

A: *It may well be that part of the reason children's contact with Dad breaks down is because going somewhere out of their neighbourhood every weekend to be with Dad in his bachelor environment becomes a bit meaningless, especially as a child gets older, and friends and sporting* *activities become more important. Some dads have their own weekend activities and expect their kids to fit in with them, because they need their weekends to be like they used to be. This can make children feel unimportant and unconnected with Dad's life. If weekends are truly all you've got, make that time as child-focused as you can.*

Shared parenting allows each parent substantial time with their children, during which they have full responsibility for day-to-day decisions about them. There is no 'major care-taker' or 'custodian' of the children, no 'part-time' or 'visited' parent. Time-sharing may be equal, fifty–fifty, or something approaching that. *Both* parents share responsibility and authority for their children's upbringing; *both* are acknowledged to be equally important for the emotional, intellectual and physical life of their children; *both* have the duty to foster their own and each other's healthy and meaningful relationship with their children.

Have a radical rethink

'Equal time-share', 'fifty-fifty', 'joint residence', etc – whatever you call it – may not be the best, most practical, desirable or affordable solution for all sorts of reasons. But there's no reason why your starting point for planning how you organise yourselves shouldn't be a 'level playing field'. Your children are your equally shared responsibility, after all. This was your starting point for family life as you planned and expected it to be, and separating shouldn't and doesn't need to change this. Try not to allow what's been the pattern in the family up till now to limit what might be possible going forwards – in other words, keep an open mind. Whatever's happened between you to result in separating, however angry and resentful you might feel about it, your kids need you *both*, and preferably not with one of you having greater control of their lives, with the other marginalised and 'put out to pasture'.

> *'If you have to divorce, this is the best possible way to look after your kids. Being involved in every aspect of the kids' lives – sickness, school, friends, birthdays, etc. – is wonderful. And they like it that way.'* JACK

So start thinking about parenthood continuing as fully as possible for both of you, however it seems to be divided on the calendar; about the scope for engaged parenting developing in new ways; and about what changes (in attitude and output) you're going to have to make if shared parenting is to work well for your children. This book aims to help you do just this.

Successful shared parenting means:
- putting your children's welfare ahead of your own feelings
- believing that your children love and need two parents
- recognising and accepting that everyone is different, and different in their parenting
- working out a parenting plan that is creative and flexible, and
- keeping at it through thick and thin.

It *can* work, and children today will benefit enormously if there's more of it. But it will be challenging.

A few guidelines for making it work

- You'll need maturity, easy-goingness, tolerance, commitment, confidence, a genuine child focus, a sense of detachment about what happened to your relationship (so it isn't still preoccupying you).
- If you both have similar value systems and are from similar cultural and economic backgrounds, there will be fewer sources of difference and competitiveness between the households, and therefore fewer adjustments for the children to make at changeover.
- The two households need to be geographically close to each other. It requires a great deal of capital to maintain two homes suitable for ordinary life, but they don't need to be equally well appointed.
- Parents' new partners and their children need to be introduced sensitively and gradually.
- Infants' time away from important caregivers needs special consideration.
- Children need to have been encouraged to be independent, both emotionally and practically. You can inspire their self-confidence by supporting their natural right to form independent relationships with those important to them, and by letting them be

responsible for practicalities they are capable of
managing.
■ Be creative, involved and accommodating of your
differences!

Jill says: I've talked with many couples who started off
quite uncertain about a time-share arrangement, but got
used to it after a few initial difficulties. It requires a lot
of trust and a lot of 'letting go'. One parent was pleased
when his daughter discovered his neighbour's child had a
similar arrangement and both kids were going to be next
door to each other in the same week.

Michael says: It's amazing how widespread it is now.
The child of a friend of mine told me that several of his
classmates are doing well in shared parenting regimes.
Interestingly, in almost all cases the parents themselves
had designed the arrangements without any help or
interference from the legal profession or courts.

Key messages

◆ Separation disrupts the familiar family pattern and calls for a new one to be established.

◆ Separated parents must face big changes and be open to new ways of doing things.

◆ Shared parenting is usually the best post-separation arrangement for both parents and children.

◆ With shared parenting, both parents share the responsibility more or less equally.

◆ With a bit of effort, patience and consistency, shared parenting *will* work.

2 Benefits and challenges

· · · · · · · · · · · · · · · · · ·

E very family is unique. At separation, each will have
its own strengths and weaknesses and its own special
issues, complex and challenging or relatively straightforward. Whether or not you have more than your fair share
of special challenges, we encourage you to retain your
responsibility for your family; to think and plan with your
partner what separating is going to mean for your kids; to
take advice from reliable sources; to use counsellors and
mediators if you get stuck; and to be open to the idea that
you may learn a lot that's useful from reading parenting
manuals and attending parenting courses. As we noted in
Chapter 1, it doesn't necessarily come naturally – especially
for dads, who've been on the sidelines for generations when
it comes to childrearing.

'I stayed a long time in a difficult marriage worrying about how the children would cope with only seeing their dad at weekends, thinking this was the usual pattern when you separate. It took a while to get our heads around the possibilities of doing something different, but Dave was able to rethink his working hours, so he could have some weekday involvement.'
Sascha

Getting advice

Many parents think they're supposed to go straight to a lawyer to be told what to do when they're separating. It's natural to think you need to protect yourself, find out your rights and start thinking of yourself as an individual who is unable to rely on partnership in the same way any more. But *you* know your children, and *you* know their parents. So think about why you're asking a stranger how to look after your children. What *you* work out as a parenting plan (see Chapter 8) is likely to be what works best for them. Lawyers are useful if you have to get adversarial, but don't go there unless you *really* have to. Most specialist family lawyers do encourage self-responsible shared parenting, and aren't always conflict-enhancing. But remember, lawyers don't know your partner or your children, and they aren't trained in child or family psychology. In addition, they may be somewhat jaded by having to deal with really polarised, difficult clients, and so may be too ready to swing into adversarial strategies, unwittingly discouraging cooperative negotiations.

In many countries – including several US states, Canadian provinces and northern Europe – there are moves to go further than merely setting up mediation services to discourage litigation for family problem solving. Non-adversarial, multidisciplinary tribunals and easy-access information centres for parent education are now in place. Mediation, conflict-resolution programs and counselling have been shown to be successful in assisting separated parents to develop the attitudes and skills that enable them to become cooperative parents.

> *'We were doing okay – talking about the kids, even having dinner together, and I was spending a lot of time with the kids. Then we went to our lawyers, just to get some advice and see what we had to do about the divorce. Wow! Everything changed! I got a nasty letter from her lawyer, making all sorts of demands. I went around and asked her what was going on. She said her lawyer told her this was the way it was done. She said she didn't know all the nasty stuff would be in a letter.'* COLIN

Doing it yourselves

Over half of separated parents have successfully sorted out their own post-divorce arrangements with little or no assistance from lawyers. How have they achieved this?

- By talking reasonably to one another.
- By accepting that they are parents, not partners.

- By getting as much information as possible.
- By seeking help from mediators and counsellors.
- By learning to put their children's interests ahead of their own.

Patterns of separated parenting are changing. Be creative and open-minded about what's possible in your unique family. As you'll know by now, we think that children need lots of real time with both parents, and that for far too long fathers haven't been spending enough time with their children, whether separated or not.

> '*I downloaded a parenting agreement from the Internet, mucked around with it and gave it to my wife. She changed it so much that we couldn't agree, so we took it off to a mediator and he helped us knock it into shape. We'll have to review it next year as the kids are young and things change. But it's working okay for now.*' PAUL

Let's now look at the main reasons why shared parenting can be the best family arrangement after separation.

The benefits

There are many benefits to shared parenting, and it's reassuring to know that they *can* outweigh the challenges that may pop up along the way.

Sharing encourages cooperation

Cooperation between parents is an enormous plus for children, and shared parenting encourages cooperation, because you can't share without cooperating. Neither parent feels left out of the family and everyone is happier, especially the children. They can cope with their parents' separation, and even with their parents not liking one another very much. But children like to see their parents *doing the decent thing* and treating one another in a respectful and reasonable manner. They like to see them sorting out problems themselves within the family.

Sharing promotes amicable solutions

This is another important benefit of shared parenting: it keeps parents out of court. It promotes non-adversarial problem solving by requiring parents to talk to one another themselves, or with the help of a mediator, and to reach agreements that suit the whole family, rather than having a solution imposed by a judge. As discussed, involving lawyers and courts is expensive, time-consuming and often traumatic. Children pick up the tension from their parents and find it sad and disturbing. They can cope with occasional blow-ups, but consistent and long-lasting conflict is seriously damaging to children.

Sharing fosters financial responsibility

There is reliable evidence that parents who have good relationships with their children pay more child support. Poverty is one of the more serious risks that children are exposed to after the separation of their parents. Lack of contact with an estranged parent is linked with lack of financial support. This, together with shouldering the major burden of raising the children, can make life difficult for the full-time mother. Shared parenting allows parents to feel that they are sharing the burdens and the pleasures of raising their children. They both know what their children are doing, they can see what they need for their education and development. They understand what it costs to provide a good upbringing for their children, and they are more inclined to be financially responsible.

Sharing ensures that neither parent is more or less important

With a shared parenting arrangement, there's no 'primary carer' or 'custodial parent', as we explained in Chapter 1. Rather, the children live with and are cared for by both parents in turn, who start thinking and behaving as *jointly and equally responsible for the children in different ways at different times*. So we can abolish terms like 'custody', 'access', 'parent visits', 'residence', 'contact', etc. This helps children feel they are attached to *both* their parents, rather than to one 'major' and another 'lesser' parent.

Q: I think he only wants shared arrangements so he can avoid paying child support. He's not really going to be there for the children, and my teenage daughter will end up doing lots of housekeeping for him. What should I do?

A: There's a formula for determining child support obligations, which is partly based on nights of residence per year and partly on capacity to pay. What does your daughter think about how a shared arrangement will work? If your fears are well founded, then your children may soon get bored. In this case you probably need to see a mediator to try to untangle the possible relationship between your ex-partner's parenting preference and financial considerations. Maybe your daughter will urge him to get some domestic help if she's feeling over-obliged to help. Maybe he'll do more than you think now that he's responsible for his own domestic space.

Sharing helps separated fathers stay involved ...

There is a great range of attitudes among fathers. Some, whether they recognise and admit it or not, seem to have developed or grown up with the idea that fathering is an optional activity; that close involvement with their children is something that they and their children can do without. Others see themselves as family- and child-minded, but don't actually do much parenting, being a presence but not an emotionally engaged one. Others again may see themselves as child-focused and be as engaged as they possibly can.

But regardless of Dad's approach to parenting, seeing his children only once a fortnight will make him feel *outside* the family, like a spectator on the sidelines. Even in families where Mum stayed at home to care for the children and Dad was highly involved in a job, Dad's position and influence was recognised, defined and accepted by the whole family. After separation, however, occasional contact with Dad often has little meaning for children. It feels like compulsory visiting, nothing like family life. Fathers, feeling the shallowness and artificiality of the experience, lose confidence in their fatherhood, lose heart and withdraw. And so they drift into estrangement. This isn't good for Dad's mental health, and is even more problematic for his children. In contrast, shared arrangements give fathers hands-on time with their children, which means real closeness can develop, with obvious rewards.

'Sometimes I do get a bit bored over at Dad's, but I like seeing my cousins. My Gran sometimes says things about Mum and I don't like this. She takes over a bit with the motherly things that Dad doesn't do, and that's really nice.' KATE, 11

Q: Do alternate weekends with Dad and Thursday nights for dinner provide sufficiently valuable parenting opportunities?

A: *This traditional pattern – whereby the kids live with Mum and go to Dad only on weekends and perhaps one weeknight – has been accepted as the norm for so long, as if it's somehow of proven value. In fact, it can create problems for both parents: it can allow Dad to have all the fun, leaving Mum to deal with the hard stuff; and it can cause Dad to feel that this is all his ex-partner wants for him, and that it can't be enough. Instead, Dad could come* up with a range of plans to discuss with her that give the children more time with him, and he could let her know that he really doesn't want to leave all the hard stuff to her. If either parent wants to insist on weekends only, the other shouldn't agree to it, suggesting instead a variant on a weekend, like Thursday afternoon till school on Monday, or after Saturday sport till Tuesday morning, etc.

... so children don't lose out

All the research indicates that children hunger for the love and attention of their fathers, and are deeply affected when they don't get it. They fail to understand what's happened, sometimes blame themselves for the situation, and are desperately sad. This can seriously damage a child's wellbeing, affecting not only their self-esteem, security and scholastic achievement, but also possibly leading to feelings of loss and abandonment.

> 'I simply couldn't face the thought of going 12 days without seeing the kids and then only having them for two days, feeling like strangers. And knowing there was her new partner with them every day ... It was easier to turn my back on it all and move on without them.' CHRIS

Important links with Dad's relatives can continue ...

If a father is discouraged from remaining or becoming involved, there are other consequences for mother, father and children. A child may be cut off from the father's family – the grandparents, uncles, aunts and cousins on the father's side. In addition, a decent and positive relationship with her ex-husband and his family can be of enormous support for a mother.

... and fatherhood can become more involved and rewarding

Shared parenting presents a great opportunity for men to become better fathers. As we've said, for too long fathers have been the *earners*, expected to work long hours to support their families while the nurturing of children was left to mothers. The gradual development of family-friendly workplaces and the growing appreciation of father-involvement in the home and family is helping to change this. Fathers need to be willing to admit that if they haven't had a lot of *hands-on* experience with children, they're going to have to pick it up quickly. They should be open to the idea of consulting their ex-partner, their own mothers and sisters, attending parenting classes, reading books, and turning themselves into fathers with real capacity and expertise. This will be reassuring for mothers, wonderful for the children, and very rewarding for fathers.

Sharing can help mothers

By dividing the parental time commitment, shared parenting gives mothers more time off to further their education, to work hard to advance a career, or to simply enjoy some leisure time. Mothers with shared parenting may be less stressed and therefore better parents and workers: they have real time to look after themselves, knowing that their children are with someone important to them. Their other parent is in touch with the children and is a dependable presence in their lives, minimising reliance on costly paid carers. Both parents benefit by being involved in the children's lives and in decisions about them.

Q: Is it right to consider a shared arrangement so that I can have childfree periods to devote my full attention to work? Will my children think I've abandoned them?

A: Shared parenting gives mothers better breaks and can enable them to get on with careers, etc. more easily. Work is a reality of life that can be your personal creative outlet as well as a means of supporting the family. Shared parenting plans that are explained in consultation with the children will most likely be understood and accepted after an initial adjustment period. If you find they complain about the time you've agreed they have with their father – as if they're saying you've done the wrong thing – try not to feel guilty about this. Mothers are frequently torn by conflict between what they are 'supposed' to do, which is always put children first, and other parts of their lives they want to develop. Encourage your children to enjoy new ways of hanging out with Dad now that you're separated and see how it goes. Remember, kids will often dump irrational expressions on a trusted parent, so don't read too much into what they say, but keep a watchful eye on how things seem to be going.

In a word ...

Shared parenting exposes children to their *whole* world – the male and the female worlds of the two most important people in their lives. Lengthy periods, including days and nights, in both homes offer the children the rich experiences of different household routines, associations with different relatives and friends, and exposure to differing parenting styles. When children spend real time with two parents they have a sense of security in two places, not just one. The two households offer an expanded network of support.

The challenges

If we are realistic, we are dealing with a difficult situation, so any means of dealing with it – even the best possible solution – is going to have some built-in challenges that will have to be managed.

Sharing has challenges for mothers ...

Mothers have to face major changes, too. They need to realise that despite their sense of guilt about leaving, or their outrage and hurt at being abandoned, or their deep disappointment in their partner, they have a responsibility to face what's happened head-on in the best way possible for their children. They must change their attitude to themselves, their ex-partner, their children, and to the relationships they have with them. Mothers tend to be the 'mediators' of family relationships, including father–child relationships, in intact as well as in separated families. The great responsibilities of parenthood begin with the exclusive biological experience of mothers during pregnancy and childbirth. This sets up mothers to feel they are primarily responsible for their children. So they usually worry about the effects of their divorce on the children – perhaps more than dads typically do. They are anxious that the children's lives are not radically disturbed or changed.

... who can sometimes have trouble sharing

Later, this natural concern can sometimes take unhealthy forms. A mother may become so protective of the children that she limits their contact with their father in his new home and with his new partner. Or, to compensate – in her own mind – for the separation, she might feel obliged to remain a full-time mother and stop or reduce work outside the home. Sometimes she sets unrealistic parenting standards for herself and the children's father. She may not trust the father to look after the children according to her standards. If one child is an infant and the father has not had the experience of much hands-on parenting, the mother will be worried about how the baby will fare. The primal nature of instinctive maternal care for the very young is difficult for some to understand, and may be hard for some fathers to feel a part of. And maternal protectiveness may seem exaggerated if she is feeling hurt and abandoned by her partner leaving the marriage.

'It's easy to be nice for a week. You're so busy catching up and being loving, you never get to the real deep issues with your kids, the ones that make you close

*– except during holidays, in about the third week.
I guess month-on, month-off might help this … If
you asked me about week-by-week sharing, I'd say
– selfishly I guess – that I'd rather have them with me
more of the time, just because I love them.'* RUTHIE

A few words of warning

Shared parenting *doesn't* work for children when:

- there are very high levels of intractable conflict between the parents
- the parents are more focused on their own entitlement to time than on the real interests of their children
- it's a regime imposed because the parents couldn't come to an amicable arrangement, and they lack the goodwill to make it work
- a parent has plenty of time technically with the children in their care but is not really there for them: the children feel unsettled, or like visitors, when a parent is inattentive – they do not feel 'at home' in both households, or
- there is inflexibility about the arrangements over time.

We'll say more about parent versus child priorities in Chapter 6.

Shared parenting will be extra challenging if:

- you're often irritated, exasperated, hurt, angry, busy or inconvenienced. If you can manage these feelings, it may be a plus for your children, but difficult for you in terms of the huge effort required to communicate and cooperate.

■ you're overly worried that agreeing to a shared arrangement will make the children feel you've abandoned them, because you've always been a daily presence in their lives. This isn't an easy feeling to deal with.

'I had to get used to amusing myself a lot of the time when I was with Dad. He was often watching the footy. I used to wish I could go back to Mum's because she spent more time with me and I felt more important to her.' JOEY

■ you heartily disapprove of many things your ex-partner is doing with his or her life and resent having your children so affected by them. You may genuinely feel concerned that you're doing the wrong thing by the children in agreeing to a shared arrangement. *Distinguishing between real and imagined anxieties when planning responsible parenting is a major challenge.*

■ you feel a duty to have more time with your kids than you can really find, and then feel bad that you haven't been more available for them when they are with you. Or, conversely, you really wanted to be with your kids so much that you took on more time with them than is turning out to be feasible, and you've ended up feeling you don't give them or your work the input that both these responsibilities demand of you.

■ you felt under pressure to agree to a shared arrangement that turns out not to work for some reason, or wasn't ever going to be right for the kids. There may then be difficulties in changing the arrangements because it involves your ex-partner giving up some time with the children, and (s)he is not receptive to your views about the children's needs.

'We had a week-about arrangement, which I was never really happy with, and I let myself be bullied into it. The kids seemed okay with it, but after a few years I felt they were really wanting more time with me. But I couldn't persuade their dad. He was quite sure they were happy with the arrangements, but I knew they couldn't tell him they weren't.' JOANNE

■ you don't know what the future holds work- or relationship-wise. If one of you wants to move, it may mean that equal or close-to-equal shared parenting is no longer going to be feasible. Deciding which parent the children are going to spend more time with if there's to be a move may present difficulties. It's probably going to require a commitment to stay in the same neighbourhood as your ex-partner, or else reasonably close. Shared parenting requires sustained commitment, which you both need to think hard about before making.

■ you have a financial settlement ahead of you that is causing uncertainty and maybe sensitivity about the eventual outcome. It's going to cost more to have two homes adequately equipped for extended parenting periods.

■ you don't want to have anything to do with your ex-partner and feel that all this cooperative co-parenting just isn't for you.

■ extended periods of parenting are frankly unrewarding and encroach on your freedom to explore new job opportunities, to travel, etc, or

■ the 'on-again', 'off-again' nature of shared parenting is difficult to adjust to, leaving you feeling unsettled and disjointed.

Once you've contemplated all we've outlined here in order to challenge any preconceived ideas you may have about separated parenting, take a long hard look at what's going to work for your children, for you and for your ex-partner. Take into account how your separation has affected both of you adults, your capacities, your ambitions, your attachments, your attitudes, the children's ages and temperaments, financial constraints – what you're really up for as far as *being there* for your kids is concerned.

Relationships for life

Through all the challenges, don't lose sight of two fundamental truths:

■ Children of separated parents do better if they have flexible, frequent and meaningful time with both their parents (which is also true in *all* families). Research shows that the children who adjust best are the ones who don't lose a relationship with a parent because of a separation.

■ The meaning in a parent–child relationship comes from what they do and say to one another when they are together. It largely comes not from the 'fun' times but from what goes on when a parent comforts a child after a fall, prepares food for them, reads bedtime stories, bathes and helps them dress. These everyday, very ordinary actions are the glue that bonds parent to child and child to parent. It takes time, availability and repetition to make the bonding strong.

Michael says: Too many fathers leave it all to their ex-wife or -partner. It's up to fathers to learn the skills of real, hands-on parenting. They should also lobby for more family-friendly workplaces. With modern office systems and means of communication, it's not necessary for most men to be at their desks all day and half the night while mothers tend to the children's needs.

Jill says: You can't just gloss over the sense of loss that changing your family means. However much you know that your life will be better when separated, you're doing something that you didn't set out to have happen, and your children certainly don't want it. However much you're hurt by him/her having left, you've got to do what's best for the kids: try to imagine what it's like for them and do the right thing. Your ex-partner may not in your eyes deserve your open-mindedness and goodwill, having chosen this path, but your children need you to give them this.

Key messages

◆ Get help if necessary: seek professional advice, check out courses/programs, read books (see the 'Helpful resources' section).

◆ If you and your ex-partner are on decent terms, you *can* do it yourselves.

◆ The benefits of shared parenting far outweigh any negatives: fathers stay involved and supportive, and mothers can get on with their lives.

◆ With shared parenting, both parents are equally important.

◆ Facing the challenges and dealing with change is essential to a successful shared parenting arrangement.

◆ Children of separated parents do better if they have flexible, frequent and meaningful time with both parents.

3 Popular myths

In this chapter we unravel some common myths about shared parenting and establish some realities. Sometimes separated or divorced parents are keen to work out a good shared parenting arrangement but are discouraged by the prejudices of friends or professionals. This chapter is intended to help those parents get past such objections.

'I sort of knew Mum and Dad were going to have to separate, and I worried about what this would mean down the track, having to see them separately. I was really hoping they'd just tell us how it was going to work out. It seemed to take forever for them to actually split and in the meantime they were just never with us together.' ANTHONY, 10

Myth #1: Kids need to spend most of their time in one stable home

Reality: This is an understandable leftover from our hopes that our marriage would thrive and our kids *would* be in one happy home. It's also an unquestioned presumption put about by many lawyers and counsellors. But it's a view that seriously underestimates the adaptability of children and fails to appreciate what is really important for them after the separation of their parents. The stability that children need is more than geographical stability. It is *emotional stability*, i.e. the stability of meaningful, continuing relationships – especially the stability that comes from knowing that both parents love them and will be part of their lives, wherever they live. Constant conflict and competition between parents about how things should be done is obviously undesirable. Having one household as the 'primary' home probably works better when this is happening, but which one should it be? Should it necessarily be the one they're used to, to avoid more change? *Or should it be the one where a real effort is made to foster the children's relationships with both parents and others who are important to them?*

There's an even broader picture to consider. The emotional stability that's critically important for a child's healthy development comes not only from ongoing relationships with two loving parents, but also from the child's wider community. A child's sense of self derives in large part from knowing that he/she has a place in the world – a real world made up of the community in which they live and grow, the homes of their parents, relatives and friends; the school, the cinemas, the shops, the sports fields they frequent, and where they meet friends, teachers, coaches and others. And more importantly, the child's world is that bundle of relationships that arise from all those physical associations and the sense of groundedness and belonging that all these important connections bring to the child.

We now live in a mobile society. This can create challenges for any child, but especially for a child in a separated family already burdened with the loss of united parents. You sometimes hear people who use the *stability* argument against shared parenting being quite able to contemplate taking children out of their communities to different towns and cities; to different schools; away from relatives and friends; placing children in childcare for long periods of time; being looked after by grandparents, boyfriends and babysitters; or sending them to boarding schools for periods of a week or a term. But they remain resistant to the supposedly unsettling idea of the children spending regular blocks of time with each of their parents, without questioning their own logic, or recognising the inherent contradictions.

'We now have seven years' history of shared parenting. The children have never felt that they did not have two homes. They know they have two parents who love them. We are not jealous about them or our homes.'
LIONEL

Myth #2: Kids need to know where they live and not be to-ing and fro-ing

Reality: A clear, simple parenting plan plus goodwill and positive attitudes from both parents will quickly get children into a routine that will become part of their daily lives. Flexibility and compromise are always valuable, but to begin with it often works best to stick fairly closely to your 'start-up' arrangements while everybody is getting used to being separated. Parents need to be on the ball, active and enthusiastic in their promotion of the plan. Hiccups need to be ironed out with a minimum of fuss. Regular reviews are a good idea, and not just when there's a problem. Breaking up a week or a fortnight into smaller chunks may mean that parents don't have to go so long without seeing their children, but it may also mean children are constantly on the go, always having to think of where they're supposed to be. Handovers are often the hardest time, so when you're planning, lean towards a pattern that has the fewest change-overs, except for very small children. The challenges of to-ing and fro-ing can be minimised by having two sets of everything (one in each home) and having regular days of the week associated with one home or the other. Having drop-offs to school and pick-ups after school can make the changeover easier for children.

Q: Surely my child will feel totally unsettled by the major differences in lifestyle and attitude we have. No sooner are they settled with me than they have to gear up to change over again. Is it better if the children stay in one place and the parents rotate?

A: *This can work well, and needs a dependable communication system to assist with smooth changeovers. If the idea is for them to stay in the family home where they have been living, this may only be possible for a time as the home may have to be sold for your financial settlement, at which point you'll probably both be getting a new place to live. Maybe you should initially consider two- or three-week blocks of time to allow for a proper settling- in before they have to uproot themselves.*

Myth #3: Infants under three should not spend nights away from their mothers

Reality: This view depends on the outdated 'attachment' theory and is contrary to recent research. Attachment theory, first researched several decades ago, tended to emphasise the exclusivity of the maternal bond and its continuity as being crucial to healthy emotional development. It was argued that a child of approximately 18 months to three years was likely to show unsettled behaviour if separated from their 'primary carer' for any length of time. This has led parents and advisers to conclude that a child under three should not be placed for the first time in the overnight care of someone away from a major carer, usually Mum. But many children nowadays have multiple attachments to important carers from a very early age and will be confident and settled with any of them, provided they are not separated from any one of them for an extended period. There is no consistent evidence that a night with their father is going to harm a baby or toddler, though individual circumstances are relevant. And if the children are well attached to the other carer (Dad), they should soon become used to him coming to them at night if needed, and doing everything else required. There is growing evidence that overnight stays in infancy form a meaningful basis for parent–child relations from an early age.

Sometimes it is Mum's needs and insecurities that make her reluctant to 'surrender' her baby to the father for more than an hour or two. At times her 'attachment' is communicated to the child and prevents a sensible parenting arrangement. Maternal anxiety is a very powerful protector of young infants and therefore deserves respect (see also Chapter 2). Overnight contact with babies and infants (approximately up to 18 months) is not in itself crucial for cementing parent–child bonds; daytime contact periods are the building blocks for introducing overnight contact later. Young babies are more settled (and their carers therefore less stressed!) if usual routines can be adhered to fairly closely, whoever is in charge.

Q: Surely it can't be right for our 12-month-old to be away from me for long periods even though he knows his dad?

A: *If he has had a fair bit of time with his dad during his life so far (with or without you being present), then* *he will have an attachment to his dad that means he's quite okay for increasingly long periods without you in Dad's care. Keep Dad informed about what routines you have established, not so as to make him feel he needs parenting lessons, but so he can respect your routines and have a settled baby to bring back to you, which will enhance your confidence in his care. An infant protesting about separations from one of you may need confident persistence, so he soon learns that leaving you does not interrupt that relationship permanently. See what periods are possible and extend them gradually. If Dad only wants a few hours several times a week at this stage, that's enough to sustain a growing attachment that can be built on later as your child gets older – even though you might want longer breaks now. Some dads aren't that good with babies on their own, so let his relatives help if they're local.*

Myth #4: The more homey, hands-on parent is better equipped to do most of the childcare because they're more in touch with the children's needs and feelings

Reality: Not necessarily, though this parent will have confidence and experience. Emotional bonds are created and strengthened by being available and doing things with and for children, but it's not just this. It's listening and talking empathically with your children, hanging out together, sharing parts of your life with them, helping them learn to discover independently and so on, that creates bonds, not how many hours you spend doing meals and school pick-ups.

Children need time to do ordinary things with each parent, not just fun things on holidays and weekends. Just because your failing partnership and your work and/or other interests kept you away from home and hearth before you separated, that doesn't mean you're not important to your children. As we've seen, a silver lining to the disappointment of separating is that children get the chance to develop a closer relationship with a parent who is committed to shared parenting but who wasn't very available to their children before, and who can therefore develop their parenting skills more effectively. A parent who appeared to contribute little to family life deserves the chance to become a more involved parent, and children should not be deprived of the chance to forge a new, closer relationship with a parent if separation makes this possible.

Being open to this may naturally be hard for a parent who has geared their life around being pretty much a full-time parent and who isn't confident that their ex-partner has the necessary experience to care for the children adequately.

'The lawyers would not entertain the idea – they ratcheted up the antagonism. I wanted to be a sole mother, and the court made orders for contact every second weekend. But my husband refused to accept being a weekend father. So eventually I gave in and we bought apartments near one another and started shared parenting. It's been for the best.' JAN

Myth #5: It's not the quantity of time that counts, it's the quality

Reality: The cliché of 'quality' time is sometimes used by judges, lawyers, mediators and counsellors to console fathers who spend limited time with their children. What you do with your time together certainly matters, as we pointed out in Chapter 2. Authoritative and engaged parenting creates emotional bonding between father and child, which contributes significantly to the child's wellbeing. These are two important elements of quality parenting. When a child senses that their father has clear and fair rules for them that are mostly consistent (i.e. he is authoritative), they feel safe and secure. And when a child feels close to their father (i.e. engaged with him) they feel better about themselves, do better at school and have fewer behavioural problems. Exactly the same thing could be said of mothers, of course, who may spend hours technically 'with' their children, but not actively engaged in parenting. If you are simply unable to spend any more time with your children than you do now, then there's even more reason to examine the quality of what you do when you are with them. A father in a shared parenting arrangement who is in fact often quite disengaged from his children, for whatever reason, is not going to build a meaningful emotional bond with them just because he is 'putting in the hours'. But common sense and logic tell us that a close parenting relationship demands lots of time!

Myth #6: **Where there's conflict between parents, there should be little or no contact**

Reality: People often seem to reach for the easy solution to conflict/contact problems. For example, a mother finds that she and the children are upset over incidents on changeover between her and her ex-partner – perhaps a heated exchange over money or a late return time. She jumps to the conclusion that the way to handle this is to limit contact. But the problem isn't usually with the time they've had with Dad, it's with the changeover. Money and punctuality are adult issues that affect the children because they are being involved in them when exchanges take place between parents in their presence.

Or a father finds that every time he sees his ex-partner she complains about the way he looks after the children, and does this in front of them. He decides that the only thing to do is to reduce his contact time with the children. Again, it's the handover that needs looking at, and it's parental communication that is the problem. Minimising the frequency of handovers and/or not having direct contact with one another at drop-offs and pick-ups will safeguard the children's wellbeing.

Professionals – lawyers and counsellors – also sometimes suggest that the only solution to ongoing conflict between separated parents is to reduce or eliminate contact between the parents themselves, and sometimes between father and children, or to have handovers supervised. This conclusion is inconsistent with research, which shows that good contact arrangements result in reduced conflict between parents.

In the face of parental tensions at handover, children often tend to align themselves with one parent, seeming to imply that the other parent is the one at fault. However, this is a potentially misguided assumption as to what the child's behaviour actually means: it confuses the picture for parents and their advisers, and so should not be the basis for any alteration of your arrangement. Rather than seeing hostility as a disincentive to shared parenting, it would be better to view it as an indicator that a better parenting plan is needed.

Sadly, there are some cases where, at least in the short term, more serious action is required. Where the incidence of conflict or violence is ongoing and serious – such that it impacts significantly on the children, and remedial action is unsuccessful – then strategies to keep mother and father away from one another, and to manage contact in a different manner, are clearly called for. Parents should take steps to eliminate serious and repeated conflict, especially when it is clearly damaging to their children. They need to learn to manage their communication, if not in a friendly way, then at the very least in a business-like manner (see Chapter 10).

'In the early days there were lots of arguments. But we gradually got into a pattern and it all fell into place. Sometimes it's better to ignore problems and deal with them later – many problems are passing or are the result of looking too far ahead.' MARION

However, 'conflict' – like 'violence' – is a broad term. It can indicate anything from raised voices to serious violence –

verbal, emotional or physical. There is a certain amount of conflict from time to time in all human relationships, and children can cope with this as well as adults. After separation, it's tempting for parents to place demands and expectations on behaviour that are unrealistic and unreasonable. They are often sensitive and anxious about the children, and therefore extra-ready to criticise or to see things their children do and say as worrying. They may subject themselves and their children to a level of scrutiny that they never applied when they were together, and which is not applied in even the happiest of homes.

Myth #7: Shared parenting works only when parents can collaborate

Reality: This is not necessarily true, although effective parental collaboration is always desirable. It's a pity if lawyers, judges and counsellors discourage shared parenting when collaboration is lacking, because it may discourage parents from trying to develop better collaboration, or from embarking on shared parenting with a clearly mapped-out parenting plan that requires minimal collaboration. It also contributes to the myth that shared parenting is not desirable just because judges don't tend to make shared parenting orders. But this is simply because judges only make orders in highly contested cases, where parents are engaged in bitter, drawn-out disputes where shared parenting is unlikely to work for the children. This is not the same as saying that because judges are reluctant to make shared parenting orders, shared parenting is not desirable. Professionals sometimes assume that the problems they see in the cases they deal with are typical of the majority, but there is a whole world of parenting styles that they seldom examine because parents who have a successful plan in place don't need professional help. See Chapters 7 and 8 for more on collaborative and parallel parenting.

Q: Is it unrealistic to expect estranged parents to have the coordination and cooperation necessary for continuity? How important is continuity anyway?

A: *We've argued that in terms of coordination and cooperation you can't have too much of a good thing. Separating may mean you're a bit short on this, at least to start with. But you* can *be coordinated and cooperative if you're really concerned about your children's welfare. Accept your differences and try to cultivate a kind of communication that recognises them. For example, if you're worried about something that you don't think Dad will even be aware of, try some self-responsible communication like: 'I know you'll think I'm a worry-wart, but could you please remember something for me so I can sleep at night? Sam really has to stick to that diet regime for another week before we see the specialist again – and do you mind if I email you again tomorrow with a reminder?'*

In this way, you accept that you have a conscientious approach to what you're trying to do, and you ask him to help you rather than suggesting he's slack and/or disrespectful about your priorities. Children can quite readily adapt to interruptions to continuity between households, so differences should not in themselves discourage sharing. However, if collaboration is in short supply, please refer to what we say about 'parallel parenting' in Chapter 8.

Michael says: It's important that parents challenge the conventional 'wisdom' because so much of it is based on precedent, folklore, unfounded assumptions and prejudices. And there's such a variety of advice being given, it sometimes seems as if we're not supposed to know how to use our own creativity and common sense! Parents need to recognise that while it might seem easier and safer to follow established rules, the best solution may come from ignoring the advice and following their own instincts.

Jill says: I really applaud people seeking good advice and becoming as well-informed as possible before making important decisions, even though parents really know their own children and their own circumstances best. Sometimes parents have to accept that there is no exact or perfect answer, that family life often falls short of ideals, and that we're all just trying to do our best in challenging circumstances.

Key messages

◆ Myths need challenging and realities need facing.

◆ Children need two homes when they have two separated parents.

◆ Organise the program to suit your circumstances, not vice versa.

◆ Infants require special consideration when part of a shared parenting arrangement.

◆ Shared parenting allows both parents to be hands-on.

◆ Both quality and quantity are important in parenting.

Some ifs and buts

. . . .

Having explored some of the common myths, let's now consider some more topics that often come up and that are important to think about before you get into your real planning. They are designed to challenge your thinking constructively, to help you recognise your areas of misinformation, and to question your attitudes and possible biases.

Children's wishes

'I was very sad when Mum told me Dad was moving out. I didn't understand why he had to and I felt he was walking out on us. But I see him pretty often and we still do the same things together although I often wish Mum was there too.' ADAM, 6

Children can't possibly know what arrangements are going to be best for them, even if they might *seem* to know what they want. Children should have their views taken into account so that they feel listened to and taken seriously, but not so that they feel major decisions are being made by them, or left to them. When it's about how much time they spend with one parent and the other, asking them to express a preference is asking them to choose between their two parents. This is a dreadful position to put children in, unless both parents are very friendly and you can all discuss it together. If you can do this, congratulations. Children who seem to be saying they want equal time with their parents are usually saying they want to be fair, even if it doesn't really suit them. Don't mistake this expression for a rational, thought-out judgement.

So, care needs to be taken in involving children in separation planning. Younger children are probably best told what start-up arrangements you parents have worked out for them when you tell them about separating. Listen to their comments (including any protests and upsets) and confirm that you have thought it through with their best interests at heart and that you're going to see how it works for a good period and see how everyone fares. Speaking authoritatively will reassure them that their parents are still working as a team, are in charge, and can tell everyone what's expected of them. Older children will want to have more say in arrangements as they grow into taking charge of their own lives in all sorts of ways. (See Chapter 6 for more on children's wishes.)

'We've had an evenly shared plan for three years now
– they accept it. They don't like moving from one house
to another, but they know that's the way it has to be
if they are to have two parents. They didn't like their
world being disrupted, nor having less money.' ANNE

Parental differences

Children will adapt to quite different regimes if you rein-
force each other's differences as parents and allow a settling-
in period at the beginning of their blocks of time. Your
differences as parents are not reason enough in themselves
for not wanting a shared arrangement. A mother and father
with different parenting styles can complement one another
effectively. As long as you have an efficient system for
informing one another (see Chapter 10) of relevant events
and how you handled them, it won't matter if you deal with
things very differently.

For example, if you allowed them to stay up late the night
before they go into their mum's care, and you know she's
stricter than you are about late nights, advise her in a considerate way that they were up late, acknowledging your
differences on this point. This can help a lot with the exas-
peration she might otherwise feel about having to manage
cranky and unsettled children, because you have shown
some consideration of the possible effects on her of your
different policies about late nights; and it will help prevent
the children feeling Mum's tension over something you've
let them do. Your kids are half you, half him/her and have a
right to experience and make sense of your differences

without undue tensions between you about them. Children living with both their parents together have to do this too, remember. You don't have to pretend to agree with what goes on in the other household, you can just say how you want to do things in your home. And don't go into too much explanation about why, or you will invite challenge and debate in response.

'Sometimes they'll tell me about what Dad does or doesn't allow. I say: "I'll check this out with Dad" or "That's his way, not mine." The new wife introduced new discipline – I talked it through with them. We negotiated it.' KAREN

Q: Does having two parents involved in everything just highlight for the child their differences?

A: *It can do, if either of you is making a big deal of the differences. Two parents together in a family are different, and each has different things to offer children in the way that they each approach life. Highlighting differences isn't necessarily bad: children learn to deal with and respect them. It is criticism by one parent of the other that's difficult for them to handle. An example of non-competitive handling of differences would be to say to your child: 'If Dad was deciding this, he'd do it this way, but my take on it is this ...'. This conveys a certainty and a familiar acceptance of your differences as parents.*

Letting them go

Getting used to having significant periods without your children is a difficult adjustment for involved and attentive parents. You may be tempted to think they might want to tell you something, they might think you've forgotten them; you might need to say goodnight, or you need to be available for them 'in case'. You need to be really honest about *who* you are keeping in touch for. There's a fine line between keeping light-heartedly in touch and over-intruding. If you are really sharing parenting genuinely, then you don't need to check they're alright – doing this conveys uncertainty to your children. And you don't need to be informed about where they are or what they're doing every moment of their time away from you. They don't need to be worrying about whether you're alright without them, either. If something exciting happens, of course they'll want to call and tell you their news. You may miss saying goodnight every night because you always used to, but they'll be fine without your call.

Parents often think that no news or overlap between homes is because children are being prevented from communicating. But it may just be because they're fine, or because they quite unconsciously manage their two homes with useful boundaries between them. With longer periods away from your children, like holidays, make some arrangement about occasional contact that conveys trust and light-hearted interest, not self-interested surveillance! More on this in Chapter 10.

When to go to court

Many parents have very profound feelings about their situation, which definitely need a helpful outlet, but no-one *needs*
a day in court. Try and be honest with yourself about motives
that are not completely child-focused but that have more to
do with punishment, entitlement, vengeance, etc. Think
long and hard about what outcomes the court could come
up with and whether any of them would in fact help the
children, or just create another set of ongoing issues. Only
if you have exhausted all possible avenues for a self-
determined solution, and there are very serious child welfare
issues at stake that leave you no option, should you go to
court. Court-imposed decisions should be a last resort in
very extreme cases. Going to court is unpleasant and traumatic, and emotionally and financially draining. Cases can
drag on for months or years. Litigation exacerbates conflict
between parents and increases pressure on children (see also
Chapter 2). Children pick up on continuing parental conflict, and it can have seriously damaging consequences for
them. It isn't good for children to know about lawyers, affi-
davits, oaths, lies, parents trying to outwit and discredit one
another about them, being assessed about their loyalties,
and so on. This isn't what family life was meant to be about.
Self-negotiated decisions in families work better and last
longer than externally adjudicated ones, and there are many
other ways – all less stressful and less expensive – to settle
disputes.

Equal influence/Equal time

Even if you see your child(ren) *much* less than they see their other parent, you *can* still be close if you're doing meaningful, engaged parenting. If you can have more time, it'll be even better for them. But time-sharing shouldn't be a competition. What do we really mean by a 'balanced' upbringing? If it's a case of both parents needing to have the same number of hours with the children to have an equal amount of input, it's likely that you're being over-focused on fairness, as if you feel uncertain of the strength of your parental input; or that you're competing with the other parent for maximum influence; or that you're so critical or concerned about their input that you want to moderate it by maximising your own. These are not usually truly child-focused reasons for wanting equal time. The things about your ex-partner's influence on the children that you're concerned about are going be in the children's life whatever the time-share arrangement you have. And there's no guarantee that having equal time will affect how much influence you or the other parent has on the children. Your strongest influence on your children's development will be because you have lengthy periods with them during which you do a range of constructive things together.

Q: Does more traditional separated parenting, with its clearer demarcation of responsibilities, reduce interparental competition?

A: *It's not the plan that produces the conflict. Indeed, a good plan can protect the children from damaging* parental competition. We think the clearer demarcation of responsibilities may be a default preference for some dads because they don't want to upset their ex-partners by taking too many established responsibilities from them. He can give a lot of support by keeping in touch with what's going on in a 'traditional' arrangement, but if he can find more time to be actively involved, he (and she) can find a way to be uncompetitive about parenting. Some counselling and parenting programs can be of great assistance here.

Creativity and open-mindedness

Parents worry about minimising the disruption to their children that their separation is going to cause, but this shouldn't lead them to assume that Dad should go live somewhere else and Mum simply carry on as she has been doing. In intact families, although fathers may spend more time at work than at home, they are still very much part of their children's lives – and on a daily basis. They are with them every day and every weekend in the ongoing interactions of family life. This valuable connection that exists while he's part of the family can't happen in the separated family. The whole character of the family changes, and maintaining both parents' engagement with family in the new circumstances needs a creative approach.

Divorce can be a trigger for improved relationships between children and parents, especially fathers. Just because Dad didn't do much hands-on stuff with the kids before doesn't mean he can't start to do more. He'll want to do this to keep in touch, and he'll be able to if you (Mum) encourage him, unbiased by your frustration that he didn't do more before the separation. Just because he now lives somewhere else doesn't mean he can't come around to pick up the kids and drop them at school, for example. Children can adapt to changes readily if these changes are explained to them with confidence and optimism.

Ideas for keeping both parents in touch with the kids

- Attend weekend sport whether or not it's 'your time'. Keep a respectful distance from your co-parent if they're more comfortable with that.
- Take an 'early mark' once a week to see the kids, hang out for a couple of hours, then drop them off.
- Get involved as a volunteer with something they do every week, whether it's 'your week' or not.
- Encourage your children to be independent, helping them learn how to get what they need from whichever parent they're with.
- Negotiate ways that you parents can help each other with transport, meetings, etc.

'Kids adjust – they are flexible. They can deal with and conform to different rules in different households. They're cunning at times – they'll try to play you off against each other and manipulate you. But we don't make a big deal of this, and often it just goes away. There are no more arguments about parenting than when we were together.' BRENDAN

Rights and responsibilities

On most issues, where there is a conflict, parents must put their children's interests before their own. Children have rights and parents have responsibilities. Parents have these responsibilities once they have brought children into the world, and it is a child's right to have responsible parents. But parents have rights, too. Each parent, together with their children, has the right to a happy and peaceful life as an independent person, consistent with their family responsibilities, but not overdependent on, or overdefined by, their worth as a parent. Moreover, every good parent has the right to participate in the lives of their children. A parent has the right – through time, activity, influence and association – to provide his or her child with the opportunity to grow and learn and develop as a person. Sure, this right can be lost if a parent is abusive, physically or emotionally violent, neglectful or immoral. But in ordinary circumstances and in the great majority of families, parents are valuable to and for their children, and they have a right to be with them and to enjoy them. But just being a parent does not confer upon you an entitlement to 'have' or 'be with' them ahead of other child-centred considerations such as their emotional needs. You are not 'entitled' by virtue of mere biology to have the care of your children for a given portion of time unless it is in their best interests.

Paid care or parent care?

Is it better for the kids to be looked after by their mum and dad (or another close relative) than anyone else? If they have to be minded during their period with one parent and if the other parent is available, should the available parent step in and take over? This is quite often a thorny issue. Let's imagine a dad who is becoming self-employed and can (at last) have flexible working hours, and a mum who has a part-time job. Dad wants week-on/week-off but is going to have to have the kids in after-school care on two days a week, which happen to be days when Mum isn't working and could pick them up after school. Mum is keen not to farm out the children too much, especially if a parent is available. Dad, for his part, thinks the kids quite like after-school care – and anyway, sometimes his mother will help instead.

It's likely that these two parents have quite different ideas about their children's progress towards independence. They may have different ideas about shared parenting. While it's true that parent–child contact is especially precious in busy, working families, it does often work better if Dad does things the way he thinks works best during his time, and Mum does things the way she likes to in her time, keeping what actually happens in each family respectfully separate. If Mum and Dad are getting on well, it may work okay if Mum does the after-school pick-up in Dad's week, but going home to Mum's place may affect the kids' continuity with Dad. Dad's working hours are a reality of his life, and after-school care is often fun, or may be substituted for time with a relative on his side of the family. There are no clear rights or wrongs here; whatever the parents can agree on will probably be okay – and can always be tried and reviewed.

Q: If one parent has to work full-time and the other works from home or doesn't work, how do you deal with the after-school care arrangements?

A: Depending on how you view after-school care (as fun or as a very poor substitute for home life) and how many helpful friends, relatives and neighbours you have, it may be best if the majority of the full-time working parent's time with the kids is at weekends, even though weekend time isn't representative of real life. See what can be done to negotiate a few early marks at work even if it's only a couple of days a week – some employers are starting to get a bit more real. Often some 'dovetailing' between parents works. For instance, if you're doing week-on/week-off, it could be good if the kids see their less-limited-by-work parent midweek, so you can work late that day, then get a neighbour to have the kids another day, and get an early mark another – which means that you're nearly sorted, without fobbing off your children too often during your busy week. Work is crucial, and children know and respect this.

Jill says: It's very important, when you feel exasperated about your ex-partner's parenting priorities, to take a step back and ask yourself: how much does what you're worrying about really matter, and what will be the real consequences of it for the children, anyway? Worrying excessively about things you can't change is very debilitating.

Michael says: Having a serious think about the difference between rights, responsibilities and entitlement when it comes to parenting is a worthwhile exercise. You can apply your thinking to the 'ifs and buts' we've presented here. Be careful, for instance, not to allow your outrage at the breakdown of your relationship to make your thinking become unhelpfully rigid and possessive.

Key messages

◆ It's vital to listen to children after separation and divorce.

◆ Different parenting styles are okay.

◆ Getting used to living without the children can be difficult at first, but you have to let them go.

◆ Stay away from court if at all possible.

◆ Uncompetitive parenting is the best way forward.

◆ Be creative and open-minded in your approach.

5   Sorting out your motives

· · · · · · · · · · · · · · · · · · ·

The single most crucial factor for successful shared parenting is whether the two of you are genuinely approaching your parenting responsibilities from the children's position. *Are you really being honest with your-selves about who shared parenting is for?* As we noted in Chapter 2, recent research into shared parenting suggests that it works for kids if it's managed in a child-focused way but not if it's managed in a competitive, adult-focused way. This is an extension, in a sense, of the established principle that parental separation is not in itself automatically dam-aging to kids, but that bad parenting definitely is; and that parents often get entangled with their own feelings about the break-up at the expense of good parenting.

But what do we really mean by 'parenting in a child-focused way'? And how do we know when we've got this wrong? Let's look at some of the attitudes and expressions that reflect a less-than-child-focused approach to separated parenting, and then you can take a really honest look at yourself with a list of questions designed to alert you to when you're in danger of not staying on track.

How your own feelings can interfere

'I know Dad's really sad about what's happened.
When he cries, I feel sad too and I wish I could fix it
for him, so I give him a lot of hugs. But Mum is a lot
happier and that's good.' CLAIRE, 7

Children are happiest when *their* needs rather than the needs of their parents take priority. If children sense that their parents want a fifty-fifty time-share because each can't bear the thought of the other parent having more time, the children feel more like possessions to be fought over than people to be loved. It is therefore obvious that it's *the relationship between the parents that is the key to the children's happiness.* When parents are in competition with one another about the validity of their grievances, it's difficult for them to distinguish between their own and their children's needs; they become inappropriately protective and/or controlling, and transmit their feelings about their child's other parent directly to the child.

Many parents face separation with a sense of injustice and outrage at what's happened, and with anxieties about the future. These sorts of powerful emotions affect your attitudes and behaviour quite profoundly, often without you realising it. Under the guise of wanting what you genuinely believe is in your children's best interests, you are expressing your own anxieties and insecurities through anger and vindictiveness. When you are destabilised by a partner leaving, you often protest by demanding fairness ('You left the family, it's not fair to take the children too!'). You unwittingly assume your children feel the way you do – abandoned. Your partner is leaving *you*, not the children, and (s)he needs your help to show them they aren't themselves being rejected.

Some parents have fears (usually unrecognised) of becoming less important to their children, and see spending equal time as the only way to retain their place in their children's lives. This is in fact a disguised form of competitiveness: you are behaving as rivals for your children's affections.

> *'For years I couldn't talk with my wife about her wanting to separate because I was just terrified of the prospect of losing touch with the children. It was as if it was an absolute certainty that this would happen when we split. Eighteen months after we eventually did separate, I realised I had developed a much better relationship with them than I'd ever had before.'*
> Anthony

Sometimes child support obligations are a factor, though it's offensive to most of us to admit financial considerations are directing us. But you may not like the way your money is being used by your ex-partner, and if equal time means no money needs to flow to him or her, you'll be happier. You may also be afraid, or may hope, that whoever has more time with the children will somehow be entitled to continue to occupy the family home.

Some lawyers advise separating clients not to leave the matrimonial home until they have obtained agreement or court orders on all issues in dispute. This may be a useful tactic but it can place enormous strain on both parents and children. *Parents with their children's welfare at heart will find a better way to sort out living arrangements.*

You may have deep-seated, unacknowledged anxieties about separating from your child(ren) that are really more about your own fear of loss, of feeling peripheral, 'on the outer'; about fearing that your child thinks you're secondary to their other parent, and not needing you; about wanting to have as much influence on your child as their other parent, so as to feel confident about them; and about wanting to prevent your child feeling you've left them. You might doubt your own position as a valued or 'proper' parent unless you have equal time. You may feel guilty that you've not been very involved as a parent till now, so you're afraid that you won't be missed and that the other parent will be preferred. These feelings are normal as you journey through your own emotional adjustment to separating, but they are largely about your own lack of confidence in yourself. They may have links to deep-seated aspects of your personality that are connected to, but far precede, your adult relationships. Recognising these feelings for what they are and how they affect you now, perhaps through personal counselling, will improve your own emotional wellbeing. This will also help your children thrive: instead of worrying too much about you, they can get on with their own childhood – as they should.

> *'Shared parenting is a means to an end. It's important for the boys to know both parents, and I didn't want to be the wicked mum/witch, seen as depriving them of time with him. But I realise how powerless I am to have any influence when they are with their father. Mothers have to get past that and let go.'* Brenda

You may want to retain your children out of vengeance (e.g. what sort of influence is (s)he on the kids, having had an affair?). You may want to punish your partner for their withdrawal of affection towards you by insisting the children must be with you most of the time even when your other commitments don't make this very practical. Or you may be unable to contemplate letting the children have substantial time away from you because you feel doing so somehow supports the behaviour of your ex-partner that you so disapprove of.

Why these adult feelings matter

> *'My wife had an affair, which I'm sure started before we separated. I was hurt, of course, but my big issue was and still is that doing this was a selfish and*

irresponsible way to deal with being unhappy with me and an appalling example to our girls, who have had to get used to the idea that their mother destroyed the family.' MIKE

All these are frequent motives for parents feeling anxious to be equally involved and, while many of them are understandable, they are really about the parents' needs and feelings, not the child(ren)'s. We're not saying you shouldn't feel these things, just that you need to know how they affect your attitudes, your thinking and your ability to compromise and be flexible. Most importantly of all, these powerful feelings can cloud your perception of your children's real needs, preventing you from being child-focused. If not addressed, they are likely to interfere with successful shared parenting arrangements. In other words, we're back at our starting point: it's not how the time is divided, or in what 'percentage', 'ratio', or 'proportion', it's how cooperative and mutually supportive your relationship with your 'ex' is that determines whether your arrangements will work successfully for your children. Children need to feel settled and at home in both households, not constantly on guard about sensitivities emanating from their parents' relationship so that their rightful place in both homes is a regular source of controversy with one or other parent.

'Separated parents have to get past hating and focus on the children. They must avoid "buying them off", getting "in with them" through regular treats. You've got to think of the children, not yourselves.' ELAINE

Checking out your feelings

Have a serious think about whether you feel any resonance with the following statements and the feelings that may be behind them:

'I'm angry that (s)he left me, and that (s)he's already got someone new. (S)He doesn't deserve to be with the children after what (s)he's done.'

'I must counter his/her influence on the children.'

'I must make sure the children like us equally, that's what's fair to them ...'

'I don't like the idea of another man/woman seeing my children more often than I do – they've been through enough already without having to get used to another person as well.'

'I don't like the way his partner brings up her children and I don't want mine influenced that way. They're unruly and disrespectful.'

'It is my duty to be there for my children at least half of the time ...'

'It's not fair on the children unless they see me half of the time ...'

'I can't have a proper influence on the children unless ...'

'He left me and wants to take the children away from me as well; he broke up the family.'

'Why shouldn't I call by and see the kids just because it's not my week?'

'The kids will be totally confused if they don't have one place they call home.'

'I have a right to see my children, they're half mine so I'm entitled to.'

'I have to pay for their upkeep, so I should have a say in how much I see them.'

'I hate asking for permission to see my children, so fifty-fifty would help me feel I have my fair say over things, that she's not in charge of where they are, rationing my children out to me ...'

'She won't ever let the children see me in her time, even though they say they want to sometimes ...'

'He keeps on setting up things so they want to see him for something or other in my week.'

'I refuse to be just a weekend dad! I'll miss them dreadfully during the week and I can't give up all my own weekend stuff!'

'I know he doesn't really want shared parenting, he just wants to be difficult!'

Behind all these expressions are motives like lack of confidence, vengeance, retribution, outrage, lack of control, need to control, a sense of entitlement, self-centredness, anger, anxiety, rivalry, etc. They reflect adult-centred priorities. If you think you identify with any of these expressions, spend some time questioning and reflecting on how valid they really are for you, and if you have a trusted friend, run your thoughts past them.

'When I hear Mum or Dad talking about "their time" with me, I feel they're competing, like I'm some kind of possession. I don't really think of my connection with them being measured by hours or days. They're different people and we do different things together which take different amounts of time.' AMY, 16

Now we're going to ask you to do a self-check. Think carefully and be as honest as you can. There are no right answers. The questions are designed to help you decide what's going to work for you and your children. It won't hurt for you to do both the mum's and the dad's list, as there's quite a lot of overlap.

Checklist for mums

1. Are you worrying overly about the children being bored or neglected with their father? Might he not have hidden talents?
2. Are you perhaps assuming they experience their father the same way you experienced him?
3. Are you anxious about them resenting you for sending them to Dad's for more time than you think they want or need? That encouraging them to feel they have another home away from you is somehow rejecting them?
4. Are you anxious about missing them too much, as they've been such a full part of your daily life for so long?
5. Are you judging his parenting capacity by how he behaved as a father in the marriage? Can you entertain the idea that this may have been associated with your relationship and how you were both managing it, and that it doesn't necessarily reflect a lack of parenting skill or, at least, parenting potential?
6. Are you anxious about 'letting go' of your children, afraid they might have too much fun or maybe even not want to come back to you? If he has family, a girlfriend, maybe other children, and you're on your own, might you feel uneasy about them comparing happy family time there with how it is for them in your home?

7. Are you ready to stand up for your way of parenting, without knocking his?

8. Are you ready to receive dirty clothes, torn uniforms and bad-tempered, unsettled, exuberant children, without showing your frustration to them?

9. Are you afraid of not being important to your children if you don't have majority time?

10. Have you got the skills and application to be all things (to your children) some of the time, as distinct from being some things to them all of the time – the disciplinarian, the detached authority-figure, as well as the warm and fuzzy talking-feeling carer?

11. Can you confidently bring to his attention something about the children in a style that's helpful, not directive?

12. Are you able to give your children the freedom to negotiate their own individual relationships with their dad, independent of your doubts, fears and naturally protective instincts?

13. When they make comments about what goes on at Dad's place, are you able to light-heartedly listen, and not engage with them over what you think about it?

14. Do you think you're going to be able to deal with major differences in parenting practices in a way that supports both your and his way of doing things, even if you heartily disapprove of his, without engaging the children in comparisons?

15. Are you worried about the child support (i.e. financial) consequences of him having more than a certain amount of time with them?
16. Will your confidence as a parent be undermined if you have 'minority' time?
17. How would you feel if your child said they wanted to see Dad less? Or more?

'I'd like to spend more time with Dad, but I know my mum would be hurt if I said so. Dad gives me a bit more freedom and we do action things together. I think Mum might be a bit jealous, and a bit lonely when I'm not with her.' JAMIE, 12

'Mum tends to quiz me about my time with Dad as if she's worried about Dad not being a good enough parent. Sometimes if I tell her about what time I went to bed or what movie I saw, she gets really cross, and I feel I shouldn't have said anything.' SAMMY, 14

Q: He's left and wants to involve his girlfriend with our children already. Surely they've been through enough without having to spend time with the person who caused our break-up being a mother to them?

A: *It's always a good idea to slow the pace of family changes so as to respect everyone's feelings. You can ask* *him to delay her involvement because there isn't any hurry. Their time with Dad is supposed to be just that. But he's likely to think it's because you have a problem, not his children. One of the great challenges of separated parenting is one parent having a valid view about something to do with the children's feelings, which is dismissed as self-centred by the other. If he hasn't thought of the wisdom of putting off her introduction for a while of his own accord, he's unlikely to listen to you. In addition, your children will find it harder to adapt if they're made to feel that getting to know her upsets you. You don't have to pretend that you approve of what's being asked of your children, but neither need you volunteer your disapproval. You can't really do anything about the situation, except support your children, who won't want to get to know her any faster than at their own comfortable pace. Encourage them to make the best of it, and to make sure they have plenty of time with Dad by demanding this of him. Most 'stepmums', whether they are mothers themselves or not, are likely to respect your significant position in the children's lives and the importance of their relationship with their dad; and your children will make sure she doesn't 'take over'. Remember, your duty is to raise children who respect and get on with people – it is not to demonise them to suit your own needs and circumstances. You need an outlet other than your children for expressing your very real outrage at how things have turned out.*

Checklist for dads

1. Are you really going to be able to get off work early, however much you may want to? Are you maybe taking on too much? Might the kids end up on their own more than you intended, with your eldest doing too much supervising?
2. Are you able to consider a request to go to Mum's in 'your' time with an open mind?
3. Are you really up for dealing with the emotional demands and self-centred immediacy of children, especially tired and cranky ones?
4. Are you really aware of how much domestic trivia got done when you were a family together, that you took for granted – such as bedtimes, healthy eating, music practice, laundry services and maths homework? Can you take this on? Or will your children feel the chaos of domestic disorganisation?
5. Can you receive information about the kids from their mum without automatically feeling she's telling you how to parent?
6. When they make comments about what goes on at Mum's place, are you able to listen with interest, and not debate with them about what *you* think?
7. Have you got the skills and application to be all things (to your children) some of the time, as distinct from being some things to them all of the time – the warm and fuzzy, talking-feeling feminine stuff as well as the disciplinary things, the detached authority-figure, masculine stuff?

8. Do you ever feel that you aren't going to be important to your kids if you don't have equal time? Could this be a reflection of how important you felt to them before separating?

9. Do you resent the idea of giving her money regularly, even if it is for the children, when she left you and got half your hard-earned assets as well?

10. If you let out a critical or exasperated comment about her, do you accept that if the children hear it, half of their very being is being criticised?

11. Do you think you have an open, easy-going relationship with your kids, so that if something was troubling them they could talk to you about it? Do you think if they wanted to change the shared arrangements in a way that resulted in them spending less time with you, they could bring this up?

12. If you have a new relationship going which looks promising, are you prepared to adjust your plans for the new partnership if it could help the children's situation?

13. Do you find you prefer to be with the children with a girlfriend around, or with your family, and maybe their same-aged cousins?

14. Are you prepared to be doing things in an engaged way with your kids 'at their level' fairly often, or are you just as happy when they're doing things independently at arm's length?

How did you go? Pretty challenging? Hopefully you've now got a bit more of an idea about when you're doing things that aren't helpful to your children, and about what's really driving your attitudes to your parenting responsibilities. Again, you should set aside some time to consider honestly how committed, child-focused and compromising you are, and maybe talk your thoughts through with a counsellor.

Q: My ex really indulges the children, even molly-coddles them. Surely this isn't good for them in the long term? Surely she should be a bit stricter with them? They don't seem willing to do much for themselves.

A: *A lot of mums, in dedicated devotion to their children, probably do more running around for them than they need to. This can happen because they have the time to if they're not working, or, because they're too busy to spend much time teaching the children self-sufficiency, doing it all themselves is quicker. They may feel guilty about how much time they spend at work away from the family, so when they are with the children they don't want to be doing chores. Your children are living with two different regimes, and you won't be able to influence hers much. That doesn't mean you can't gradually teach your children the rewards of contributing more to the daily round when they are with you, though they may need a lot of reminders about what you expect of them. Don't be tempted to tell her you think her way of parenting is wrong; you shouldn't need to assert to her your better parenting skills. But do* *tell her from time to time about things the children do independently that you're proud of. And don't feel that you must have equal time with them so that your parenting ways will have a prominent influence on them.*

Jill says: It's important for parents to accept that feelings interfere and obscure important issues, but that they won't always. New partners are sometimes a great help with reality checks, though of course they can generate resentment and anxieties for some ex-partners. You have a responsibility to try and be child-focused and open-minded about your parenting role, which means letting go of pursuing fairness. You're not 'entitled' to time with your children. They deserve and have a right to time with you. You won't be less important to your children just because they spend less time with you than your ex-partner.

Michael says: However valid your criticisms of each other are, you aren't going to safeguard your children from the influence of the things you dislike by making sure your children are with you half the time. It's sometimes difficult for dads to become emotional all-rounders. Young children especially want and need warm, patient and communicative parenting which, at the risk of being sexist, is not something men are famous for! Shared parenting with young children means getting better at this feminine stuff, or you may find that your child craves for Mum and feels you don't 'understand'.

Key messages

◆ Shared parenting needs to be child-focused, not adult-centred.

◆ Check out your feelings about yourself, your ex-partner and your kids – and be honest.

◆ Adult emotions can get in the way, especially if your ex-partner is in a new relationship.

◆ Being positive will help your children be honest about the arrangement.

6 Considering children's choices

'I had my views about where I wanted to spend time, but I didn't feel I could say anything about it to either of my parents, I didn't want to be choosing between them. Even now I'm older, if I drop in at Mum's work on the way home from school in Dad's week to say "Hi", I sort of don't bother to mention to him that I saw her.' SOPHIE, 14

How much you should involve your children in decision-making about shared parenting arrangements needs careful consideration. They may have views that they express, and in some families where everyone is getting on well – especially where there are older children – it *is* possible to have appropriate discussions involving everybody about how the separation is going to work, or about reviewing existing arrangements. Some research suggests that shared parenting is more likely to work when children are consulted and involved. Yes, children do like to be consulted about things that concern and affect them, but there are good reasons why care needs to be taken here.

Children are consulted today more than ever. We encourage them to express themselves confidently and make decisions for themselves. Sometimes they get their own way about things they're really too young to decide on, because today's parents are anxious to cultivate positive self-esteem and keen to be liked by their children. They equate firmness and direction with putting them down. Also, many busy parents are time-poor, and may lack the time and effort that is necessary to be patient and authoritative with their children. Supporting children, encouraging them in healthy attitudes and principles, discouraging harmful ideas and behaviour – all this takes time. A quick *yes* or *no* from a parent rushing off to work may work for the parent, but may not be good for the child.

Even if we pride ourselves on running a fairly strict, 'traditional' household, our kids are being schooled the modern way, which encourages healthy debate and questioning. They're growing up in a society that is democratic, where everyone has a right to have a voice. So our attempts to be traditionally strict are likely to fail. There is confusion today about how to be an effective parent: we are frightened to be firm, and our proper parental authority (so important to children's security) can be easily eroded by our children's energetic and often eloquent responses. Being separated is a further challenge to parental confidence at a time when major decisions requiring parental authority need to be made.

How much say should they have?

Our seemingly expressive and articulate kids can give the appearance of maturity. So we talk things through and ask their opinions, as if their ideas and expressions are well thought out. But even older children can do with direction, even though they're often challenging the rules or expressing their views vigorously. Too much explaining and talking things through is often a sign of parental anxiety and a need for reassurance. Courage and conviction need to come from the parents who head the family, particularly when it comes to managing your separation. *Some kind of compromise between giving in to your children, letting them decide things you should be more definite about, and hearing their input sympathetically while having the final say yourselves is what's required in today's families.* Too little structure, too much self-determination too early, makes for insecure and uncertain children.

'We'd had a week-about shared plan for several years. My ex wanted to review it because she said the kids weren't happy, and that they wanted more time with her. I can talk with the kids about anything and they've never indicated to me that they wanted to be with me less. I think she wanted this really and maybe made them think they had to say it to her.' KEN

Divided loyalties

Parents, feeling bad about putting their kids through a separation and anxious about their wellbeing, can rely too much on what the children say and do. They can rely too much on seeking their children's views, enlisting their loyalties, to get reassurance and approval for their own views and feelings. Separation divides children's loyalties. Each of them is half you and half your estranged partner, in character and temperament. If you encourage them, deliberately or otherwise, to express their preference for one kind of arrangement over another, you're really asking them to choose one parent over another. This is potentially damaging and will cause them to say what they think is safe and fair, not what they actually want. That is, unless your children feel confident that their parents are not in competition with one another about them. But even if they aren't worried about how their views may affect their parents, they probably don't know whether what they think they want is what's best suited to their emotional needs.

Cooperative parents should be getting together and deciding this for them, at least at the start of a separation – and certainly with younger children (say, under ten), though much will depend on sibling configuration (an only child of nine is in quite a different situation from a nine-year-old youngest of four). All the dilemmas and feelings associated with a changing family are confusing enough for us adults, and certainly what children think they want may be confused, changeable and not well thought out. Keep in mind that children caught in loyalty conflicts quite often give distorted accounts to one parent of their experiences with the other – accounts which may seem significant to you but which are not always reliable indicators of feelings and preferences.

'My parents said I could please myself, but in a way I'd rather they'd told me what they wanted, because I felt I always had to worry about their feelings and make sure I was spending about equal time with each of them just so as to be fair. I would be three or four days into a pleasant stay with Dad and I'd start worrying about whether it was soon going to be Mum's turn to have me.' DAVE,12

Children's wishes and the law

Lawyers often talk about children's wishes as if they are the deciding factor in resolving separation disputes. This tends to encourage parents to rely on, and even cultivate children's expressions and, as we've said, they may not be independent. In many if not most Western countries, the law is obliged to take into account children's wishes and not ordinarily make orders that go against them. But the law usually has in place a system whereby children's expressions are communicated to the court via an independent legal representative and a child psychologist's assessment, so that their wishes can be independently interpreted and given appropriate weight. (But the law only rules in highly contentious cases anyway, and a court is very unlikely to make an order for shared parenting because in contentious cases there is a lack of parental cooperation and/or an unwillingness to commit to a parenting plan). Involving children in counselling and mediation is a relatively new idea, and we don't know much yet about the relationship between children's involvement in these processes and long-term outcomes. US experience suggests that children, as well as adults, benefit from programs that help them cope with the changes in their lives due to their parents' separation.

Q: The children complain to me that they spend more time with Dad's family than with him, that he often uses his parents as minders. He wanted shared parenting but it seems only for someone else to do it for him. Isn't this unfair to them?

A. *Are you sure they're really complaining? They mightn't mind all that much. You might resent it, but his family is important and may well be of great help to him as he gets used to his separated parenting. If you think he doesn't spend enough one-on-one time with them, you might be able to tactfully bring this up with him – perhaps during a general review – but if he hasn't worked this out for himself, you may not have much impact. Maybe his own father didn't do much hands-on parenting, and so he didn't grow up knowing how fathers engage with their kids, in which case he feels more comfortable being a step removed from hands-on connection. Perhaps this was the kind of father he was when you were together. In any case, at least your children know they are regularly in the company of their dad and his family rather than not there at all. It's* *important for separated fathers who, though dedicated dads, have not played a hands-on role in their children's lives, to learn to do just that: to be with their children. This means arranging work so that they can spend time with them, not going to movies or sport but just hanging out, chatting, kicking a ball, cooking a meal together.*

The likelihood is that your kids say different things to each of their parents, which may be contradictory if you don't interpret them in their context. Of course, saying, 'I want to spend more time with you, Dad' doesn't necessarily mean 'I want to spend less with Mum'. Saying, 'I want equal time with each of you' doesn't mean that's actually what they want; it's what they think is fair to their parents and it will enable them to avoid expressing a preference for one over the other. Your kids shouldn't have to be worrying about diplomacy and loyalties, they should be being kids, having fun, experimenting with life within safe boundaries, free from worries about their parents' difficulties.

This doesn't mean not talking and listening to what your children do say. It does mean using their expressions as opportunities to reassure them that you're interested in what they have to say and are 'taking it on board'; that you parents are going to take everything into account and sort out what's going to work.

*'I campaigned to go and live with my father, saying
to Mum that I needed to hang out with Dad more.
He's less strict than Mum and seemed less worried
about money. Eventually she agreed, and I was happy
for a while, but I soon got a bit lonely as Dad in
fact worked long hours and I was on my own a bit,
which had seemed cool to begin with. Having lots of
takeaways was good at first, but it wasn't so "homey"
at Dad's.'* SEAN, 15

How to involve your children in your parenting arrangement

- Try and have them feel they can talk with you honestly about how it's all going for them, without worrying that they might upset you.
- Invite them to review the arrangements from time to time. Children feeling positive about shared arrangements is associated with parents who are approachable and flexible, willing to change the way the days are shared, happy about children seeing their other parent 'out of time', and able to encourage more independence about arrangements as they grow older.
- If your own gut feeling combines with recurring expressions from the children to indicate that something about your arrangements needs changing, talk with your co-parent about it (more than once, preferably, to allow for careful consideration), before

enlisting the children in negotiating anything. Keep in mind that it's likely they're saying quite different things to each of you from time to time.

- Older children will naturally want to be more independent about their lives. If they want to have contact with their other parent in 'your' time, don't be too rigid about it. They *should* be progressively taking charge of their own lives, which doesn't mean anything's changed about how they feel about their parents!

'Flexibility is the important thing. The program cannot be static. You've got to adjust for the different ages of the children, the different things that happen. Kids change, you change, times change. If you allow for that, it will work well.' TOM

Some children's comments about sharing

'Sometimes my mum says, "Do you want to change it and go two weeks-about so you have longer to settle in?". She thought I might be swapping over too often, but I reckon two weeks would be too long not to see each of them.'

'When I go to Dad's for a few days he expects me to fit in as if I was always there. My room is really his office.'

'It's okay, but I prefer Mum's place even though it's further from school and she works long hours.'

'It's a drag when you've got things at the wrong place. It was better when they organised for us to have a double set of everything.'

'My sister and I felt we had to hate Mum's boyfriend because he was with her before the separation, and Dad was outraged by this for years. Even after we felt okay about him we still acted like we didn't, to sort of "protect" Dad.'

'I prefer blocks of time, otherwise you're always thinking, where am I supposed to be tomorrow?'

'I'd really prefer more time at Mum's but I could never tell Dad.'

'Long after I left home I went on feeling I had to ring Mum if I'd talked to Dad, or it wouldn't be fair.'

'I sometimes find I say things to Mum or to Dad that are a bit exaggerated. Like telling Mum it was boring at Dad's when it wasn't.'

'I'm a bit scared of Dad. I can't talk to him about things I can talk to Mum about, even though I've tried to. But then I certainly can't mention Dad's girlfriend to Mum, let alone that I quite like her!'

'I reckon week-about is okay because we change over on Sunday night, and I see Dad at footy training in Mum's week. If I want to see Mum in Dad's week, he's cool about it.'

'When I left home, it was the nicest thing having all my gear in one place. I felt settled for the first time, after living out of a bag for years.'

'I wanted to spend more time with Dad when I was around fifteen, and I did. But whenever I talked to Mum on the phone, she made me feel I'd done the wrong thing by her. My feelings for her hadn't changed, though.'

'The hardest thing about going back to Mum's was that she always wanted to know all about every detail of what we'd done together, who visited, whether Dad's girlfriend had stayed over and stuff, like I was supposed to be some sort of a spy!'

Jill says: Aim to do more listening to your children and less talking. Listen so you make them feel you've heard. If they want an answer, you don't have to give one immediately. Ask to talk about the issue again and see what they seem to be saying then. You don't always have to have the answers, either. Don't assume what they say is necessarily independent, though it may be. Aim to be approachable and flexible.

Michael says: Being able to have meaningful conversations with children is an important part of being truly child-focused. Talking for the sake of having conversations is more of a female thing. Yet fathers could do it to good effect – there doesn't always have to be an action plan or a decision at the end of a chat! Having parents who are approachable and open-minded about the idea of making changes, as families grow and circumstances change, makes children feel valued.

Key messages

◆ Children should have some say but not too much.

◆ Understand that your children may have divided loyalties.

◆ Involve the children in parenting decisions.

7 Working out a timetable

If you're cooperating flexibly with your partner and not worrying unduly about fairness, whatever division of time you have will be likely to work. As we've regularly asserted, fortnightly father contact is undoubtedly better than sporadic, half-hearted contact, but real parenting is more hands-on than fortnightly contact allows. Fathers should seek, and be encouraged to have, much more time than the 'traditional' two days out of fourteen – in fact, at least a third of the total time. It hasn't been established that children are confused or disadvantaged by having two places they call home, though many parents feel it must be, perhaps mainly because our ideal of traditional family life has centred on one home. But having two homes doesn't mean that hours and days must be divided evenly for each home

to be emotionally significant for a child, or for each parent
to be an important influence on their child.

*'I was afraid that once we'd agreed on a plan I would
never be able to change it. I wanted to start with
four days a fortnight and build up slowly towards
the children having more time with their dad, rather
than start off with half-and-half. John was adamant
that he was "aiming" to have equal time eventually,
which worried me a bit. But after several round-
table discussions, we arrived at a compromise with an
undertaking to review.'* ISABELLE

Getting started

What governs what you decide to put in place is likely to be
your passion about your children, money, geographical
proximity, your children's ages and your employment obligations. Try to regard plans as part of a process that needs
to develop in phases as your children grow, with regular
reviews.

With both parents spending substantial periods of time
being responsible for their children, two homes are needed
that can shelter comfortably. But just like equal hours spent
in each home being overemphasised, it's another myth that
the two homes have to be equally well-appointed for the
children to have emotional stability (see also Chapter 2).
Some parents feel that the children's stability will be pre-
served if they don't have to leave their familiar home as well
as adjust to their parents' separating. Your timetabling will

be very affected by where the two of you live, and not just because of geography: if keeping the family home intact means one parent has to 'camp out' in a much more modest place, it may be more difficult for the kids to adjust to feeling 'at home' there. There are some advantages to both parents moving somewhere new, if it's all done with confidence and creativity. Children will adjust to leaving their past behind if their parents can – just as in 'unseparated' families, where the kids adjust to relocation because of employment or other factors. This is because the parents have got the move sorted out themselves and are being positive about it, including celebrating rather than covering up what was good about the home they're leaving. After you've sorted out your start-up plans, you can put them into practice while you still all live together, if you can't move straight away – provided you can find a way to respect one another's authority and separateness with the children during their 'shift'.

Separated parents should sit down with each other and analyse their lifestyles – the life patterns of each of them and of their children. They should come up with a plan that they think might work and then present it to the kids, making whatever adjustments they think are necessary. They should be creative and, above all, positive and confident about it. If they look at it with goodwill and confidence, the kids will pick up on that and it will work! *Where there's a will there's a way!*

> *'We were both determined not to let the kids suffer from our break-up. We resolved from the start that we would never fight in front of them and never say nasty things about each other. We decided on a program*

*of contact and, with a few changes, have stuck to it.
If we ever want to discuss some problem, we meet for
coffee.'* Helen

Timetabling patterns

Maybe week-about will work, maybe weekend-plus. If the
parents live some distance from one another, perhaps month-
about or term-about. But continuity of schooling is important to all parents and children, and if parents have to move
to accommodate this, then that's what should be done (if
feasible). Wear and tear on everybody is minimised if there
doesn't have to be too much regular 'commuting'.

Q: Too much to-ing and fro-ing can be an extra stress, so
shared residence is probably better in extended blocks,
but how long with each parent is suitable?

A: *It depends on the ages of your children. Week-on/week-
off seems intuitively simple and conveniently predictable
for many families, but you are the best judge of what
stretches of time they can handle away from a particular
parent. Consider a midweek interlude with whichever parent
is 'off-duty'. If the 'off-duty' parent is attending sports
training and Saturday fixtures whichever week it is, it helps
children feel connected and gives a less sports-minded
parent a break. So, once again, be creative! If geography
is a factor and if the kids' relationship with both is well
established and cooperative, longer periods will be quite*

okay with older children, but schooling and friendships will govern your decisions. Within similar educational systems, changing schools for a term or a year can be enriching for a confident child who is well supported by both parents.

Even very young children can benefit from overnight stays with another parent. Overnight parenting makes for meaningful family experiences and should not necessarily be deferred just because a child is young, so long as (s)he is used to spending days and nights away from a substantial carer. If not, care and common sense should be exercised in gradually introducing an infant to this experience. The important principle here is that enjoyable time be spent frequently – with short intervals of a day or two between gradually increasing lengths of time – with the parent (usually Dad) who has had a less continuous, round-the-clock, caring role than Mum has. Younger children as well as infants may be less comfortable with extended stays away from an important carer, so breaking up time into slots of a few days rather than a whole week may work better.

School-aged children may have better curriculum continuity in term-time if the same day of the week is spent with the same parent, though during the primary school years this is probably not so important.

'We've always been flexible. We started off with week-about, but changed to fortnight-about when he went to high school. Then, in his final year, with all the study and pressure of exams, we thought it would be

*better for him to live in one spot, so he lived with me
and visited his father a lot – that worked well.'* JO

Some parents have even tried 'nesting', whereby they retain
the family home for the children, and the parents move in
and out according to a roster. The parents move about
instead of the children, who stay in their established home.
Like both parents setting up a new place at separation time,
retaining the established home removes any feeling that the
parent who left the home is the one who 'left' the family,
because the other parent still lives there with the children.
This requires special parents who are willing to make special
efforts to be so child-focused. But it *can* work!

Other parents have found it useful to look first at the
children's after-school activities – such as sport, music and
dancing – particularly for teenage children. They then program their residential arrangements according to who can
accompany or pick the kids up after such fixtures. In these
cases, it may be that the boys can stay with Dad for their
football training, and Mum can have some special time with
the girls, or vice versa.

*'It's a 5/2 formula: Mondays and Tuesdays they are
always with him; Wednesdays and Thursdays always
with me; and we alternate weekends. This gives
continuity: the kids are in the same place for the same
event and can keep the same gear in the same place.'*
JULIE

There are all kinds of possibilities, and all of them workable, so long as the will is there to make them happen – and provided that both parents have a positive attitude to their parenting program. Too many changeovers and too much travel adds to everybody's burden. A simple arrangement helps everyone remember what's happening. Longer periods of time at one home, as children grow more able to do without one parent, allows for settling in to the routine of where they are before they have to change again.

> *'You've got to keep at it. There's no let-up – one kid's got to be here and the other somewhere else. One has forgotten his homework, and the other wants to see a friend. You've got to be really organised. But it's worth it. The kids haven't lost anything, and they are happy. We talk a lot.'* Gerry

Q: If it's week-about, which is the best changeover day? Is it best if each parent is responsible for the same days of the week?

A: *It depends on what your weekends involve. For preschool children, it makes no difference, though it may do for you. Sunday changeovers work well, allowing a chance to take stock and catch up before a new week. If Fridays are a family evening, then it makes this a good time to 're-connect'. Some families like the idea of the week at one home starting with a weekend so that the settling-in process is relaxed. Some parents find that having the* *same days of each week gives better term-time continuity. If you miss all the dance classes because they're always on Tuesdays, then you can always go to the end-of-term performance. It's also convenient for the dance teacher or the maths coach if they're dealing with the same parent all the time.*

The key parenting plan principles

Your parenting plan will be built on three principles:

1. Your belief that your children need to feel valued and loved by both mother and father.
2. Your conviction that they need to belong to their community of parents, relatives, friends, schools and favourite places.
3. Your intention to encourage one another to live happy, independent lives while being the best parents you can be.

These principles in action – some examples

■ *Two parents both working but with a certain amount of flexibility in their hours.* Here two girls, aged five and eight, have a 'a week with Mum then a week with Dad' arrangement, changing over on a Sunday evening. Because a week with one parent is quite a long time to go without seeing the other – especially for the five-year-old – they have Wednesday evenings overnight and go to school the next day with the parent on their 'off-week', to break up the week. This also gives each parent a 'mid-shift break'.

■ *A 10-year-old girl and 14-year-old boy spending seven days with each parent in turn.* With this arrangement, Dad attends weekday sporting fixtures whichever week he's on. The 'on-duty' parent sees the kids to school on a Monday, takes their belongings over to the other house, and the other parent starts their week with them after school on Mondays. School holidays are pretty much the same, with parents reviewing each year's holidays in advance if longer overseas trips need to be fitted in.

■ *Alternating weeks, different blocks.* The new 'shift' begins on Sunday morning and in Week 1 it runs Sunday to Wednesday after school for Dad; in Week 2 it's Friday after school till Tuesday after piano lesson for Dad. This arrangement means that Dad is always responsible for the Sunday evening 'wind-down' before the school week, always deals with Monday homework (including maths, which he can assist with) and does the Tuesday drop-off to piano lesson. This means that each parent is responsible for the same days of the term-time week, giving consistency. In the holidays they leave it the same unless they are going away. If a special school event occurs, both parents attend if available. If Mum wants a weekend out of town, she can ask for a Sunday from Dad (but not too often).

Q: It's the brief, everyday moments of family life that make you feel in touch with the kids. How can separated parents retain these contacts?

> **A:** *There's no reason why you shouldn't, say, pick up your son from Mum's and drop him at soccer training on your 'off' week. Or pick him up and take him back as well. It helps Mum and it gives you those important 'windows' with him. It needn't mean you are obliged to have a lot to do with Mum, you can just put it in your plan and it can happen like clockwork. And Mum could do the reverse when it's her 'off-week'. If your job doesn't enable you to have much weekday contact with your child, why not call by Mum's place and take him to school?*
>
> *If there's goodwill and mutual support, 'dovetailing' like this, across designated parenting shifts, keeps children and parents in touch with one another and actively demonstrates parental teamwork.*

- *Two-week blocks with each parent for two teenage girls who go to and from school independently*. They make their own arrangements about contacting the parent they're not with. Mum works at a business near their school, so one or other of the girls often calls in on her way home. The changeover is on Friday night so the fortnight always begins with a weekend for settling-in and a 'catch-up'. They're beginning to organise holidays themselves depending on their parents' work commitments and their own plans.
- *Week-about with the changeover around the school day on Mondays*. A nine-year-old boy attends school midway between his parents' residences but several suburbs away from each. Tennis lessons happen after school in the vicinity of school, the swimming class in Mum's neighbourhood,

and martial arts in Dad's neighbourhood. Although it's a fair drive for each parent to get him to school, this arrangement means that the boy's school community is no more associated with the mother's neighbourhood than with the father's, so the parents feel of equal standing in their son's life.

'I felt that I was giving away part of my motherhood. Some of my friends told me I was mad and it was the wrong thing to do. But Dave was a good father and the kids missed him so much that I gave in, and now they are with him for five or six days a fortnight. I ached for them at first, but it's working out okay. I can do other things. The main thing is the kids are happy.' IRENE

Jill says: Parents should be creative in sorting out these arrangements, and be 'savvy' about any protests or uncertainties coming from the children, because they probably won't be all that coherently thought out. Rearranging the family is new ground for everyone in the family. Take time to consider the various possibilities before deciding on one.

Michael says: Not only must parents be creative, they should also be courageous. I mean, they have to put aside their fears and give it a go! They should be convinced that the effort is worth it and that the kids will quickly become used to the new system, particularly when they realise they are still seeing a lot of Mum and Dad, and others they have grown up with.

Key messages

◆ Timetabling is always a work in progress.

◆ Get started by taking the time to analyse your lifestyles.

◆ Timetabling patterns can vary greatly.

◆ Consider the kids' schools and activities, your work, distances to travel, etc., then sort out a pattern to suit the family.

◆ Be creative, positive and confident.

8 Designing a parenting plan

'I think it was quite good the way they had a proper written document about us. It made us feel they'd been really serious about us, and they met together several times to gradually work it out. Now they can refer to it if there are any disagreements.' ANDREW, 15

Every family has a plan, whether it's written down or just worked out from time to time. Perhaps written parenting plans would be useful in intact families, too, but in a separated family they are extremely helpful, and sometimes essential. Not only does a good, documented plan prevent and solve disputes, it also makes life smooth and predictable. After separation, the lines of communication between parents, and between children and parents, are stretched. Living together in the same house made communication easy – arrangements could be made and changed in an instant. Geographical separation makes all that more difficult, calling for a different strategy. Even those parents who still talk to one another can't be on the phone every five minutes to change an appointment, to remind Dad to pick a child up after football training, to tell Mum that holiday arrangements have to be changed.

Family life is complex enough. Parents work, full-time and part-time, and in different locations; children attend different schools; they have varied activities and at varying times; and as they grow up they have differing needs. Separated family life is even more complex. The best idea is, therefore, to make it as easy as possible. This is what a written parenting plan will do for you.

Your own parenting plan

You can set down in black and white all the things that you both agree are important for looking after yourselves and your children from now on. Your parenting plan is *yours*. Have a look at the sample parenting plans in Chapter 9, but don't feel limited in any way. Your plan can contain as much or as little detail as you decide is necessary *to make it work*. It can state your philosophy of parenting, your attitudes to your children's wellbeing, the particular needs of each of the children, details about schools and future education, details about medical care, where each parent will live, when the children will be living where, transport arrangements, holidays, religious events, special festive days – even legal issues if you wish. Take some time about this: exchange drafts, think about it, get some advice if you think you need it, and then formalise it with your signatures.

Q: I'm a bit uncertain about how much detail we need to have in a parenting plan. She has done most of the family homemaking things all these years and I'm happy for that to continue. Should we formalise things in writing?

A: You don't have to. But a separation is an important event in a family. However much trust and goodwill there is between you, it's a good idea to 'sign off' on family life as it was, and make a clear statement of how things are going to be from now on, even if it's a fairly general one. It's a committed statement of the continuing responsibility you both intend to have for your children, and how you're both going to express this involvement. And as time goes on, as circumstances change and new partnerships develop, your initial undertakings are on record as part of the family's history.

What to include in your parenting plan

A plan might contain some or all of the following elements:

- the parents' philosophy and attitudes regarding their care of the children

- an acknowledgement of responsibilities for the welfare of the children, day-to-day decisions and more major things requiring consultation
- where everyone will live
- what time or times the children will spend with each parent, grandparents, etc.
- the importance of maintaining relationships with parents and others
- how the travel between homes will occur
- the schools and school activities, extra-curricular programs
- arrangements for holidays and special days
- special needs regarding medication, education, clothes, equipment
- financial arrangements, extra expenses
- communication between parents, sharing information about the children
- communication between parents and children via telephone, email, etc.
- appointment of a mediator/coordinator/referee to deal with disputes
- a specified time for a review of the plan, and
- additional agreements, e.g. not to discuss money in the presence of children, and so on.

'It was all our own work. We had friends already doing shared parenting and we thought it was the way to go. We are convinced it's advantageous for the kids – they're not bargaining chips, and they need to know that both parents want them. We find week-about works well, with the changeover Sunday evening. The parent without the kids picks them up (so they won't feel one parent is getting rid of them).'
Brian

Collaborative parenting plans

This is the type of plan that will work for separated parents who can treat one another with decency and sensitivity. They acknowledge the importance of both parents in the children's lives and they work hard to foster all the relationships that are important for their children. They talk to one another regularly about the children. Their children's friends are welcome in either home. In some cases they are able to come together for Christmas and birthday parties and the like. *Many separated parents are doing this!*

But no matter how well you are getting on with your ex-partner, a written parenting plan is still a valuable asset. Even in the most amicable of separated households, accidents and misunderstandings arise. People are different and sometimes difficult, and the same goes for children. Circumstances can change; unexpected things happen. The separated family is a special family, and living in it calls for a special effort. At times it's easy for the best of parents to tire, to lose heart, to feel exhausted, to wonder if their efforts are worthwhile.

A well-constructed and principled parenting plan can help you through the tough times. You can take it out and read it again. You can discuss it with your ex-partner or your children. It will help you renew your commitment, and may help renew your enthusiasm. One of the key features of a collaborative parenting plan is the commitment of both parents to consult one another on issues that affect the children, their welfare and development.

> *'We told our lawyers what we wanted and they were really good. They helped us work through all the things that we thought were needed to make life easy for the children. They also made some good suggestions. After a couple of sessions, we signed a parenting agreement and they filed Consent Orders in the court.'* SARAH

Parallel parenting plans

For parents who find it impossible to get along, 'parallel parenting' can work. That means each household has its own set of rules, and the parents have a minimum of contact and communication. The one thing that they agree on is that the children have two parents and that they are going to spend some time in each household according to a determined schedule.

The essential ingredient in such a plan is the commitment of both parents to stick to the terms of their agreement. Moreover, the plan will need to be extremely detailed to cope not only with the children's day-to-day timetables, but also to foresee and deal with expected changes and hiccups.

Where there is ongoing hostility between separated parents and little or no communication, a written parenting plan is essential. With it, and with a firm commitment to abide by the rules, shared parenting can still work. Without it, misunderstandings and confusion will inevitably arise and children will suffer.

Q: I'm finding what to do about the children's arrangements incredibly difficult to deal with. I feel so upset for them. I don't trust their father to do the right thing by them. I don't want to have anything to do with him. I don't want them staying overnight with his girlfriend there and I want him to feed them properly and stick to sensible bedtimes. Can I have all this put in a parenting plan?

A: You can have very specific details incorporated into your plan, and so can he. There's no limit to what you can have included. If you feel he's out of touch with their routines, inform him, perhaps with the help of a mediator if talking with him is very uncomfortable for you. Or write lists for him, as appendices to a parenting plan. You could suggest, for a period while everyone gets used to the separation, that he spend his time with them without his partner. Try and approach the creation of your plan with an open mind, inviting him to draw up as many clauses as he wants to. Work out yourself what sort of issues you want to be consulted on, and aim to set out the arrangements very specifically so you don't need to have much contact with him. You may be well advised to have a neutral third party as a pick-up and drop-off person, so you don't have to see him and the children don't sense your discomfort.

Making what's best for the kids work for parents, too

- ▣ COMMUNICATE   Make sure everything goes from parent to parent, not through the kids. Use the phone or email or a contact book, if necessary, to avoid confrontation or debate in front of the children. (See Chapter 10.)

- ▣ COOPERATE   You and your ex-partner no longer have to agree over who washes the dishes, but you need to agree – or at least agree to disagree – when it comes to the kids. If necessary, have separate rules at each household, and respect the differences. Kids will adjust so long as each parent is consistent.

- ▣ KEEP ROLES CLEAR   Remember: he's no longer your husband but he will always be your child's dad. Perspective counts when trying to cool easily inflamed emotions.

- ▣ GET A GO-BETWEEN   If matters get out of hand, enlist a mediator or specialised counsellor to defuse tension and to resolve disputes.

'I've found that the best way to deal with a difficult decision is to WRITE IT DOWN, and then ask myself: how is this going to affect the kids? How is it going to affect my ex-wife? How will it affect me? This has stopped me from doing some very stupid things.' JIM

Sure, there will be problems, even after implementing the most carefully structured parenting plan. Life's like that! Life in intact and separated families is never smooth or uneventful. Why should it be? Human beings – including children – and human events are naturally unpredictable and, at times, quite unreliable. People react in different ways to similar circumstances. If it were any different, life and people would be deadly dull and boring.

Flexibility

If your parenting is going to work, you have to build into your plan an element of flexibility to cater for those occasions when something just cannot happen; or, if it's already happened, that calls for a change in plans. Be flexible about demanding 'make-up' time. But, more importantly, you have to build into *yourself* an element of flexibility. You have to tell yourself that life is not always smooth sailing and easy. It is not so in intact families, so why should it be in separated families? Chill out, settle down, don't expect too much of yourself, your ex-partner or the children. Be positive, do your best and it will surely get easier.

'We've had a shared arrangement going for several years. I guess you could call it "parallel" as we don't talk much and are very different. Both of us have weekday time with the kids and I think it's important to be involved in their schoolwork as I'm a bit stricter than their mum. When she wanted to move to the other side of town, we weren't able to work out a compromise because we'd never been able to talk, and I didn't want to give up my weekdays. I was happy for her to move, but not take the children.' JIM

You may want to formalise your parenting plan and make it legally binding. This may make you feel safer and more 'signed off'. It means that if your ex-partner does not abide by the terms of the agreement you can lodge an application in court. In most jurisdictions, you must have your plan written in the form of a legal document so it can be lodged as 'Consent Orders' in the appropriate court. But of course this still allows you to vary the orders by mutual agreement without having to go back to court.

Examples of both collaborative and parallel parenting plans are set out in Chapter 9. You'll note that there is little difference in the essential elements of each kind of plan. But in the parallel plan you will see less warm language and a stronger emphasis on sticking to the rules and to appointing a really good coordinator. The promise to attend a parenting program is particularly important in parallel parenting situations. If nothing more, separated parents who do not communicate with one another should see the parenting plan as a means of making life easy and reducing unpleasantness.

Jill says: It's sometimes assumed that parenting can't be shared unless Mum and Dad are communicative and cooperative. Obviously, parents getting on well is ideal, but parallel parenting can mean shared parenting is possible with minimal communication and with different parenting styles. Children can cope with distance and minimum communication between their parents, provided everything's sorted out, set down and adhered to.

Michael says: The great value in committing your arrangements to paper is that it sets out in black and white your commitment as decent and sensible parents to look after your children and yourselves after the break-up of your marriage. It tells your children and the world that you're taking this seriously and that you're going to measure up to the responsibilities that parenthood brings. It proclaims your belief that your separation does not represent a tragic failure and that family life is finished. Rather, it announces your firm intention to care for your children while getting on with your own lives.

Key messages

◆ Every family needs to commit to a plan.

◆ Your plan can include all the details you each need.

◆ Collaborative parenting plans are for parents who can talk to one another.

◆ Parallel parenting plans are for those who find communication difficult.

◆ What works for the kids will work for the parents.

◆ Above all, be flexible.

◆ If you wish, you can formalise your plan at court.

9 | Sample parenting plans

· · · · · · · · · · · · · · · · · · · ·

Here are some sample parenting plans, to show the range of detail possible. It's up to you to negotiate what you want in yours.

Sample collaborative parenting plans

Collaborative Parenting Plan A

This is a fairly simple one, suitable where there is reasonable communication and collaboration between parents.

The following is the agreement reached between John and Liz Smith in December 2005, concerning the shared parenting arrangements for their daughter Jane (aged 18 months):

John and Liz will share the responsibility for Jane equally.

Her time is to be spent substantially in the care of her mother, with liberal time spent with her father commensurate with her age and emotional development.

In the immediate term this will operate with Jane spending each Tuesday evening from approximately 6 p.m. in her father's care, overnight until Wednesday morning.

On alternating weeks she will in Week 1 spend Thursday evenings with her father from approximately 6 p.m. approx until 8.30 p.m. or when she is put to bed by him at her mother's home; and Saturday overnight, commencing Saturday afternoon and extending into Sunday as agreed.

In the following week (Week 2), the Thursday night as described above will be substituted by Friday night overnight, and the very next Sunday she will spend the evening with her father from, say 6 p.m. until her bedtime at her mother's home.

M	T	W	T	F	S	S
Wk 1	overnight		eve		overnight	
Wk 2	overnight			overnight		eve

Until further notice, neither parent will have Jane in their sole care for holidays for longer than a few days without contact with the other parent.

Christmas, Easter and other special days are to be shared reasonably as agreed.

The above arrangements can be varied from time to time if agreed and do not exclude John seeing Jane at other times should he seek to do this.

Signed and Dated:

....

Comment: *The first two clauses express the basic principle of the plan; then 'liberal time' with John is defined across a two-week period in a way that spreads his time with Jane at regular intervals so they never have a very long period between contacts and so Jane doesn't have any long periods away from her mother. This is appropriate for such a young child, and one whose two parents have been involved in her overnight routines.*

Collaborative Parenting Plan B

Here there are three children under 10, the youngest an infant. The mother had initiated the separation and in the short term agreed to leave the home except for the purposes of parenting.

At the meetings on 3 and 11 February 2006 between Fran and David Brown with the assistance of Joan Settlewell (mediator), the following was proposed:

The three children remain residing at the family home.

David continues to reside there and be primarily responsible for the children on weekdays during term-time from 7 p.m. until 7 a.m.

Fran will no longer reside there but will have access to it from 7 a.m. until 7 p.m. on weekdays during term-time and be primarily responsible for the children during these times (see below). In the event of both parents being there at the same time, then responsibility for the children will be joint.

A room will be maintained for use by Fran for the purposes of assisting overnight when agreed.

Fran and David will plan how the weekends are allocated and agree on some minimum numbers of weekends each, having in mind that it be as far as possible equal. Fran's weekend contact will take place with the children's residence as a base, with outings arranged by her and overnight stays elsewhere, as arranged, until such a time as Fran sets up suitable premises of her own where the children can stay for weekend and school holiday contact.

School holidays will be shared as agreed. Every effort will be made to give each other as much notice as possible about plans for holidays.

Both Fran and David will seek the other's assistance in the first instance when requiring care for the children during their periods of responsibility.

Both Fran and David undertake to keep one another informed about activities and excursions involving the children so as to keep one another reasonably in touch with the children.

Fran and David will have joint responsibility, in consultation with each other, for the making of decisions about the long-term care, welfare and development of the children including but not limited to all aspects of their education, health, sporting activities, religious attendance or training, and any plans for interstate or overseas travel.

Fran will have sole responsibility for making decisions about the day-to-day care and welfare of the children during the periods they are in her care.

David will have sole responsibility for making decisions about the day-to-day care and welfare of the children during the periods they are in his care.

This parenting plan is to be implemented as soon as practicable after Fran and the children return from their forthcoming extended holidays, and reviewed six months later. In the event of significant circumstances changing before this review, it may be brought forward. These circumstances may include, for example, David finding a new partner, the house being sold, or Fran taking up employment.

If disputes arise, Fran and David undertake to settle them quickly and with the help of a mediator if necessary.

Signed and Dated:

....

Comment: *This plan recognises that Fran was the instigator of the separation and David was quite resentful of Fran's decision, and very keen not to unsettle the children more than necessary (as of course was Fran). He wanted some specific undertakings in the agreement in order to feel comfortable, which Fran was quite happy to give, even though she didn't feel she particularly needed them in there. David worked during the day but Fran at this stage didn't, so their day and night shift arrangement made common sense. You'll see that there are two paragraphs towards the end that define Fran and David's decision-making responsibilities. This makes a clear, almost formal, statement of committed intention, which is often helpful. The mention of the mediator was something they decided to put in because it was going to remind them of how they arrived at the decision – that a professional third party had assisted them and thereby endorsed the agreement.*

Collaborative Parenting Plan C

This one concerns two primary-aged children, the mother working part-time and the father full-time, with the father very anxious to have half time and mother very concerned about the kids having so much time away from her.

The following parenting arrangements and undertakings were agreed upon in July 2004:

Julie and Simon will continue to have shared responsibility for their children, Jack and Sophie, and honour the principle of meeting their need to be with each of their parents for as much time as possible, having regard to their other needs as they grow and develop.

The children will be in the care of Simon in 'Week A' from Monday afternoon until Wednesday morning, when Julie takes over their care until Friday afternoon/ early evening. Simon then has them for the weekend (beginning Friday) and until Tuesday of 'Week B', when Julie has them from the Tuesday afternoon until the following Monday.

Julie and Simon will remain committed to a principle of flexibility to accommodate their respective work and other commitments. To honour the principle of the children being with their parents in preference to other carers, each will call upon the other to assist with the children during their periods of responsibility, as deemed appropriate.

Julie and Simon will have joint responsibility, in consultation with each other, for the making of decisions about the long-term care, welfare and development of the children including but not limited to all aspects of their education, health, sporting activities, religious attendance or training, and any plans for interstate or overseas travel.

Julie will have sole responsibility for making decisions about the day-to-day care and welfare of the children during the periods they are in her care.

Simon will have sole responsibility for making decisions about the day-to-day care and welfare of the children during the periods they are in his care.

It is agreed that parenting arrangements will be reviewed quarterly, or at the request of either Julie or Simon.

Julie Jones ....

Simon Smith ....

Agreed this day (date) July (month) 2004 (year)

Comment: *Simon really wanted a week-about arrangement, but recognising that Julie thought a week without contact with one of the parents was too long, they broke the week up into shorter segments, describing the weeks as 'A' and 'B'. There isn't anything particularly recommendable about planning in two-week cycles, it's just that alternating is easier to remember and has a manageable rhythm to it. Julie and Simon wanted quarterly reviews, and you'll note that either can request a review at any time. This is important, as even if one parent thinks everything's fine and doesn't see the need for a review, if the other does see this need, then there should be a review. They are still partners, for committed co-parenting.*

Collaborative Parenting Plan D

This plan for Tom (11) and Kate (9) utilises the established 'nanny', Sharon, who works in both homes, providing some useful continuity.

This is the parenting agreement between JACKIE and MIKE mediated in October 2005. It is based on the underlying principle that Jackie and Mike continue to have joint and equal rights and responsibilities in relation to the children, Tom and Kate; and that

neither parent wishes in any way to be less involved
or associated with the children than previously,
while recognising that spending less actual time
with the children is the inevitable consequence of
the separation.

Without prejudice to the future, and with the under-
standing that the initial arrangements are start-up
arrangements for the immediate term pending review,
the following agreement is proposed.

That during school-term time:
- the children reside with Jackie from Monday after
  school through to Thursday, Sharon assisting
- on alternate weeks from Thursday after school until
  Monday morning to school, the children reside with
  Mike at his premises with the assistance of Sharon
  on Thursdays and Fridays
- on the intervening weekend, the children continue
  in the care of Jackie from Thursday until Sunday
  afternoon at around 5 p.m. or as otherwise agreed,
  when they go to Michael for Sunday evening
  overnight until school the next morning
- both Mike and Jackie have contact with the
  children during their time with the other parent as
  agreed for events such as basketball, etc., and
- when either Mike or Jackie travels on business, the
  children are in the care of the other parent and
  return to the care of the travelling parent on their

return, making the necessary adjustment to the alternating routines.

During school holidays the children are to remain in their father's care on 'his weekend' until Tuesday, or to commence their weekend with him on the Wednesday, and at such other times during the school holidays as agreed.

Neither parent is to make plans to move anywhere with the children to a distance that would affect shared parenting significantly, without consultative, cooperative, open discussion about the implications of a contemplated move.

The arrangements are to be reviewed (with the assistance of the mediator if sought by either), at least when the new year's term-time commitments are known, or sooner if necessary.

Signed and Dated etc.

....

Comment: *This plan begins with an overall statement of commitment, which often feels good to have in writing. The hardest part of making a plan is often getting the arrangement started. Parents get anxious about setting precedents, or about finding they can't* change things they've agreed to. Hence the 'without prejudice' clause. Parenting plans, of course, are about children, who grow and change all the time, so there should be a set of arrangements to get started, which can easily be adjusted once it's been tried out. Sometimes it helps to specify term-time and holiday times separately, as Mike and Jackie have done here. Note also the undertaking about possible relocation by either of them.

Sample parallel parenting plans

These are useful where there is little communication and collaboration, and arrangements have to be 'nailed down'. They can also be used for collaborative parents who like a lot of detail.

Parallel Parenting Plan A

Names ....

We, Mike and Tracy, are the parents of ....

1. General principles
Although we have chosen to live together no longer, we will both continue to be active and involved parents to our children. We have generally agreed in principle on parenting issues and intend our parenting to remain cooperative, united and consistent as far as possible in the circumstances.

We also believe that, as well as being our desire, it is in the best interests of our children that they have close and loving relationships with both of us. We agree that:
- We are both competent, trustworthy and loving parents.
- We are both responsible for the parenting of our children. Irrespective of where the children are

living, we both have a responsibility and a right to participate in significant parenting decisions, and agree to regularly consult each other and keep each other informed about parenting issues.

- We will endeavour to maintain a friendly relationship between us.

2. Naming

Our children are named Ben and Isabel, and are to be known by these names. Each of us will refer to the other as the children's mother or father. We will not encourage the children to call any other person mother or father.

3. Shared parenting

We agree to:

- consistently acknowledge and promote the special role that each of us has in the lives of our children
- regularly discuss the children's progress regarding their intellectual, emotional and physical development
- as far as is possible and practicable, to consult each other regarding the children's routines, discipline, schooling, clothes, health and welfare, and
- seek and value the children's wishes regarding these shared parenting arrangements and act on these, taking into account what is appropriate considering the children's ages.

4. Health and emotional wellbeing

We will foster good health and emotional wellbeing in our children. To ensure this we will:

- make joint decisions about our children's health and emotional wellbeing
- agree not to denigrate each other and endeavour to maintain a friendly relationship between us
- agree not to denigrate each other's interests and associations and to deal respectfully with other cultures, particularly in relation to the children
- as far as possible keep the children to their normal routines with regard to bedtimes, sleeping arrangements, clothing and general wellbeing
- ensure that our children's milestones (for example, birthdays) are acknowledged wherever they are living
- whenever possible, both attend celebrations and special occasions such as school presentations and sporting events
- keep each other informed about our children's emotional and physical health
- inform those who are entrusted with the care, education or treatment of our children of any important medical information, and
- cooperate with any remedial intervention recommended by a competent health professional.

5. Discipline

We agree to discuss and review the children's behaviour and any possible disciplinary action. We agree not to use physical discipline (hitting), humiliation or shaming and we will ensure that anyone else to whom we entrust the care of the children will also abide by this.

6. Residence arrangements

To facilitate shared parenting, we agree to live within 30 minutes' travel of the children's school. We agree that the parent in whose home the children will live, will collect the children from the other's residence. Residence arrangements will take into account weekends with each parent and the midweek activities of the children. The following plan shall commence on 2 May 2006:

- During Week 1, the children will live with their mother from Friday after school to Monday morning. The father will pick up the children from school on Monday and they will live with him until the following Monday morning.
- During Week 2, the children will live with their mother from Monday after school until Friday morning. The father will pick up the children from school and they will live with him until Monday morning.
- During Week 3, the children will live with their mother from Monday after school until the following Monday morning.

- During Week 4, the children will live with their father from Monday after school until the following Friday morning.
- This pattern will continue throughout the year unless changed by agreement.
- Otherwise contact will occur as agreed between the parents.
- On Christmas Day, birthdays, Mothers' and Fathers' Days, the children will spend at least part of those days with each parent.
- Each parent may telephone the children at any convenient time within reason.
- Each parent will participate in the children's school activities, which may include reasonable contact at the school with the children.

We also agree that:
- we will advise each other of any proposed travel or overnight visits outside the usual residential arrangements
- the parent with whom the children are living on any day is responsible for their care on pupil-free days, if they are sick, or during school or public holidays. That parent is also responsible for supervising homework and other school-related activities and extra-curricular activities
- if either parent is unable to care for the children for a period of more than 48 hours, the other parent will

be notified immediately so that we might agree on appropriate care for the children
- the children can phone the other parent at any time and vice versa (within reason), and
- we will not make any plans for holidays outside the normal residence arrangements without gaining the other parent's consent. We will inform each other of any holiday plans in advance, with suitable details such as travel times, contact phone numbers, etc.

7. Education

We will:
- ensure that we provide the best possible educational opportunities for our children and encourage them to pursue their special interests, and
- supervise and support homework, home study and practice.

Each parent has the right to participate in activities and receive information regarding our children's education, irrespective of which parent is caring for the children at the time of any school activities. We will pass on to each other any information we receive about our children's education.

8. Family contact

We agree to foster a close relationship between the children and their immediate and extended families by arranging regular visits and telephone contact.

9. Child support
We agree that we will share equitably in the costs of raising our children and that we will jointly make financial decisions about our children whether or not we each contribute equally in financial terms to their support.

10. Death of parents
We agree that, in the event of the death or incapacity of one of us, the other parent will assume full responsibility for the care, welfare and development of our children. We both agree to bequeath to the children a sufficient proportion of our estates to ensure that their living and educational costs can be met until they become adults.

11. Communication, consultation, information sharing and conflict resolution
We agree to:
- share as much information about our children as possible in the circumstances
- share information with our children to ensure that, as far as practical and in an age-appropriate way, they remain reassured that the separation of their parents has not diminished our relationship with them and that they are not left insecure about the future. We acknowledge the children's right to know about changes in family relationships and the

desirability of involving them in decisions that will affect them, such as proposed changes to living arrangements, introduction of new partners, etc., and

- resolve conflict constructively, cooperatively and in the best interests of our children. If we experience a conflict over the parenting of our children which we cannot resolve ourselves, we will seek counselling or mediation to resolve the issue.

12. Re-evaluation of the parenting plan

We agree to review this parenting plan as a matter of course, in June of each year, until we decide this is no longer required. We will also review the plan at any other time:

- as our children's needs and/or circumstances change
- as our needs as parents and/or circumstances change, or
- at the request of either of us, or the children.

For example:

- before either of us moves home
- if either of us re-partners
- if another child is born
- after a family crisis or death, or
- when each child completes primary school.

13. Acceptance

We acknowledge that we need to implement the parenting plan in both practice and spirit for the wellbeing of our children and ourselves.

We have each carefully considered the provisions contained in the parenting plan, and exercise our informed choice by signing it. We agree that we will each keep a copy of the parenting plan.

Name   Name

Signature   Signature

Date   Date

Comment: *You can see that there are undertakings about proper parenting principles spelled out in many of the sections of this plan. It can help very estranged parents who are suspicious and distrusting of one another to have these written down in detail. There's quite a lot of detail in the 13 sections, and residence is set out in a four-week cycle with changeovers around the school day, which is preferable when parents are uncomfortable with each other. The cycle continues throughout the year regardless of school holidays. Even the review clause has specific reasons set out in detail. The principle of having so many details spelled out is that it means very little has to be discussed – it's all in there.*

Parallel Parenting Plan B

This parenting plan is a formal statement of how the needs of Lilly are going to be met after the separation and divorce of her parents.

This parenting agreement covers the following important areas:
1. Residential and childcare arrangements
2. Time spent with each parent and the wider family
3. Recreation and holiday arrangements
4. Resolution of conflict
5. Education and religion
6. Health and medical issues
7. Parental responsibilities
8. Relocation of residence
9. Process to alter the agreement

The aims of this agreement
- To make residential and other provisions for Lilly that encourage each parent to maintain a loving, stable and nurturing relationship with Lilly, consistent with her developmental level and the family's social and economic circumstances.
- To ensure that Lilly spends ample time with both parents so as to allow her to develop a meaningful, not a superficial, relationship with her mother and father and others important to her upbringing.

■ To promote the amicable settlement of disputes between Jack and Kathie, which will enhance the wellbeing and stability of Lilly.

Objectives
■ To provide for Lilly's physical care.
■ To maintain Lilly's emotional stability.
■ To provide for Lilly's changing needs as she grows and matures.
■ To set out the authority and responsibilities of each parent with respect to Lilly.
■ To minimise Lilly's exposure to harmful parental conflict.
■ To encourage both Jack and Kathie to meet their responsibilities to Lilly through this parenting agreement, rather than by relying on judicial intervention.
■ To otherwise protect the best interests of Lilly.

It is agreed that because individuals' lives and children's developmental needs continually change, this agreement must be flexible and allow room for adjustment.

A definition of shared parenting
It is the intention of the parents who have agreed to shared parenting that each of them shall continue to have a full and active role in providing a sound social, economic, educational and moral environment for

Lilly. The parents agree to consult with one another on substantial questions relating to educational programs, religious upbringing, significant changes in social environment, and health care. They agree to exert their best efforts to work cooperatively in making plans consistent with the best interests of Lilly and in amicably resolving disputes as they arise, without involving Lilly.

1. Residential and childcare arrangements
- Lilly will live for one week with her mother and for the following week with her father.
- Changeover day shall be every Wednesday, unless varied by agreement.
- The parent who is to have care of Lilly for the week shall pick her up from school on Wednesday afternoon and take her back to school the following Wednesday morning.

2. Time spent with each parent and the wider family
Whenever Lilly's grandparents, uncles, aunts, cousins, etc. are visiting, Lilly is to be afforded all reasonable opportunity to spend time with them at the residence of the parent in question, so that she might get to know her extended family. It is agreed that reasonable account will be taken of the total time spent with that particular parent.

3. *Recreation and holiday arrangements*

1. Lilly is to enjoy alternate Christmases with each of her two parents, with this year being a Christmas spent with her father.
2. School holidays shall be shared, or the normal program adhered to, after consultation between the parents.
3. Lilly is to be able to have free, unhindered telephone contact with both her parents. Both parents agree to encouraging and enabling such contact to work so that it can become meaningful and free from tension for Lilly.

4. *Resolution of conflict*

If disputes or conflict arise, the parents agree to settle these as quickly as possible and without involving Lilly. They will first attempt to resolve disputes between themselves, but failing this, agree to seek mediation with the nearest available agency.

5. *Education and religion*

Both parents agree to bring up Lilly with the values and principles of their religion. The choice of school and religion is to be discussed and mutually agreed upon by both parents.

Both parents will together make the choice of school and any other major decisions for Lilly. In the event of disagreement, then the provisions made for mediation will apply. Both parents will endeavour to negotiate with a spirit of resolution rather than conflict, and to arrive at an outcome with the best interests of Lilly in mind.

The school is to be notified of this parenting agreement, and in the event of any serious problem or accident at school, both parents are to be notified.

All reports and 'parent days' and any information on any school activities or invitations will be sent to both parents, and both parents will have an equal right to discuss any issues with the school authorities, and neither will be prevented from being involved. Both parents will discuss and come to agreement on any such issues together before making any decisions.

6. Health and medical issues

The parent having actual physical custody of Lilly at any point in time shall take responsibility for dealing with medical and dental emergencies. Both parents agree to discuss the general health care needs of Lilly and to advise each other of illnesses and treatment requirements.

Any other health issues are to be discussed and mutually agreed upon.

7. Parental responsibilities

It shall be the responsibility of both parents to prevent any form of parental alienation, and neither parent will 'put down' the other parent to Lilly, but rather assure her that both parents love her and care for her.

8. Relocation of residence

If either parent desires to move out of the area, the parents must discuss this in advance and adjust the shared parenting agreement accordingly.

9. Process to alter the agreement

Lilly's parents promise to make genuine attempts to implement and adhere to this agreement for Lilly. Should one parent consider that any change or alteration is necessary, that parent shall immediately contact the other and discuss the situation.

Signed .... Mother

Signed .... Father

> Comment: *This plan starts out with quite a lot of introductory material, a statement of what the plan covers, its objectives, etc. – even a definition of shared parenting. As we noted earlier, these formal statements can provide nervous or resentful parents with reassuring reference points. Note the undertaking*

to provide Lilly's school with a copy of the plan. Also, there is no obligation to refer to the other parent for assistance with Lilly's care in 'their' time with her. This cooperative dovetailing, which appeared in many of the cooperative parenting plans, doesn't work with estranged parents, who will be communicating minimally with each other and not needing to know too much about the other's lives, such as how often they use babysitters.

Jill and Michael say: Remember, you can have as much or as little detail in your parenting plan as you like. The more detail you have in it, the less need there is to consult each other – you both know what's happening.

10 | Communicating between households

· · · · · · · · · · · · · · · ·

Throughout this book we've stressed the importance of talking to each other about planning your arrangements and managing your parenting responsibilities. Once you've got your shared arrangements up and running, how much communicating is necessary and how can it be improved for the sake of harmony and cooperation? What can parents do in their conversations with their children to help? First we'll address the issue of consulting between parents.

> *'They never said anything to us for ages, but we knew.*
> *And when they eventually sat us down, they thought*
> *we'd be surprised and shocked. We'd been expecting it.*
> *We'd overheard them talking about breaking up. It*

was kind of a relief to have it more in the open now,
but I still don't talk about it to them.' MATT, 8

Between parents

The emotional turmoil of separating parents means that difficult feelings interfere with sensible parenting. Sometimes parents just split up and *allow things to happen*. They don't sit down as a family and tell their children what's going on. And how does this situation unfold? The kids find out in fits and starts, getting differing and contrasting messages from their parents, their friends and relations. These parents don't give their children clear answers to questions about where they'll live, what's going to happen and why. They fail to reassure their children of their continuing love and involvement.

A good start is when parents both shoulder the responsibility for what's happening (regardless of who they might feel is most to blame for damaging the relationship) and take positive steps to make it work. This means having many conversations together over a period of time about all the different possible arrangements that might be good for you and your children, and about what you're going to say to them about why you're separating. You're aiming to make a concerted effort to start having different conversations with your partner now – as fledgling co-parents, no longer as frustrated lovers. And you're aiming to retain your joint position at the head of the family despite separating.

'We hardly ever saw each other. We emailed important news and information. If I wanted to make a change in the arrangements, it just wasn't worth the angst, so I always stuck to the letter. Sometimes if there was a school function Tom would ask if only one of us, not both, could go. This was sad, but I guess it was easiest for him this way. One day, I hope things will relax a bit more, but for the time being it seems to be working alright with us at arm's length, and for me personally, it's easier.' FRAN

Hints for difficult discussions

- Recognise that your concern for your children arouses very strong feelings and sensitive reactions.
- Set aside a time (an hour maximum) when there's unlikely to be any interruptions. Agree on this 'appointment' in advance to allow for you each to prepare thoughtfully.
- Choose neutral territory – a café or park.
- Agree that there are going to be several of these planning meetings because this is not only very important, it's also going to be very difficult.
- Set some ground rules together about the length of the meeting, about reserving the right to adjourn if there's a stalemate or if one of you gets too emotional to talk coherently, or to allow thinking time. Acknowledge that any viewpoint expressed or

proposal made is provisional and can be withdrawn, altered or added to.

- Don't feel you've always got to respond to your partner straight away. You can keep charge of the pace (and therefore the intensity) of your discussions if you pause and say you're going to think about that proposition or claim, and reply in due course.

- Try to summarise where you've left the issues discussed in terms of who's proposed what, what's agreed, what's not agreed, what you're going to do prior to the next discussion, etc.

'There are days when I want to just scream from the rooftops, "How did this happen, and why?" I've become a master at learning how to count to 10 when I get angry. But I don't have much choice but to behave with as much integrity and strength of character as I can, because even though the marriage has failed, we can make the divorce succeed, especially where the children are concerned.' Karl

If your meetings break down

If the two of you can't communicate productively, consider seeing a separation counsellor or divorce mediator together. If you don't know what's going to be best for your children, see a counselling psychologist who's a separated parenting expert. They may also be able to help you develop some useful strategies that will help you manage your feelings and discuss things sensibly with your ex-partner. *Do as much reading and consulting and comparing of notes as you can.* Then meet again with your ex-partner and readdress the issues.

Q: Is it 'normal' to have both directing affairs in the same area of family activity?

A: *It probably isn't 'normal' in the sense that division of domestic areas often falls into naturally efficient 'departments', presuming that parents mostly respect the way each other does things. They share suggestions, and offer back-up support. Separation can mean that because you're parenting on your own, there isn't the scope for undermining one another's methods in front of the children, but you both have lots to offer each other if you communicate about how you manage the various areas of family life.*

Make a real commitment

Once you've separated and have a start-up set of arrangements in place, stick to the rules. A 'good divorce' is possible and well worth the effort. Like a good marriage, a good divorce takes time and effort. Separated parents need to make sure they conduct themselves with decency and fairness. Keep a record of things that concern you about what everyone is doing and saying. Some of it will be of small long-term consequence, but your journal entries will give you an immediate outlet for inevitable frustrations, as well as providing useful data for your reviews. Meeting regularly to compare notes and discuss the kids is fine and fantastic, and for many it comes naturally. But if you can't do this, it's not crucial. You can co-parent on minimal communication, as we saw when considering 'parallel parenting'.

> *'It was harder in the beginning with all the emotion around the separation. But we have improved and now sometimes talk by phone or in person. Email works best for us. We don't talk a lot now the kids are older. They tend to look after themselves.'* ARTHUR

Communicating and job-sharing

It can help communication to think of shared parenting as being like a workplace shared job. When you change shifts, you wouldn't dream of telling your relieving colleague (who, like you, is fully qualified to do the work) how to do the job you share. But you *would* tell them relevant information about what had happened during your shift. And you'd have no trouble deciding what was relevant and what wasn't, what you thought was worth trying and, having taken the decision during your shift to deal with something a certain way, you'd say what follow-through you recommend regardless of how they felt about what you'd started. *There's a world of difference between being concerned enough to offer useful information about what's happened during their time with you, and being interfering, over-intrusive or insultingly directive.*

You can say what happened, what you did, whether it worked, and what didn't seem to work. The closest you should go to directing or insisting how you want something handled is a warmly expressed, 'I'd really like it if you'd...'; and if you're on the receiving end, agree to do it if you do intend to, and if you don't, just say something like, 'Thanks, I'll take that on board', or 'Sure, I get where you're coming from on that...'. For example, 'He had a nightmare last night so he may be tired today', or 'I had to take her to the doctor and this is what was advised, can you see it through, please?' Even if you think your 'ex' is a health freak and you disagree with the treatment, it's unlikely to harm your child, and it's an opportunity to be supportive and cooperative. Your 'ex' will probably ask your child whether you did it and it'll help him greatly if (s)he can say, 'Yes, Mum, Dad did make me finish the tablets!'

Q: What's the best way to handle things that your child says he/she is allowed to do by your ex but which you absolutely disapprove of? Is it okay to say you don't care about your ex's wishes?

A. *There's always a fine line between reinforcing, for your child's sake, your ex's way of doing things and appearing disinterested so as to prevent yourself coming across as judgemental! Try to keep a light-hearted, conversational interest in what your ex is saying but don't engage in what you feel about it. Just get on with doing things your way when you're in charge. If you and your ex get on fairly well,*

*next time you are discussing the children, you could say
– using a neutral, 'for your information' tone – why you
disapprove of the issue in question, and hope they take
it in.*

Communication methods

1. *Talking face to face* about the children is ideal.
2. Have a private *phone call* just before changeover.
   But when you're busy, when handovers don't
   happen directly, or when there's tension, then
   other methods may work better.
3. Some kind of *logbook* will help you remember
   things, and you can make entries as things occur,
   not just at the last minute before handover.
   Logbooks are best not left in kids' bags for general
   reading. *You* should pass it back and forth, not
   the children.
4. *Email,* of course, is very handy. You have a
   permanent record and can transmit instantly
   regardless of whether your ex-partner is available;
   and it's cheaper than endless phone calls (when
   you can catch someone at a bad moment) and
   messages left. But the written word has some
   hazards. Your intentions can be misinterpreted
   when you don't get tone of voice or body
   language. We tend to write concisely and the
   printed word can sometimes easily be perceived as

> cryptic, abrasive, directive or over-formal, creating
> sensitivities and misunderstandings.
> 5. *Fax*, though rapidly becoming yesterday's
>   technology, can be useful in the same way as
>   email, with the same advantages and
>   disadvantages.

'Sometimes I'd be ready to tear my hair out at the frustrations of trying to talk sensibly together! We both care about the children enormously, but we just can't seem to have a conversation! We've agreed to keep our exchanges to an absolute minimum and use email for the time being.' SARAH

Reviews

You'll notice in our sample parenting plans that there are often *review clauses*. Once you have an agreed plan in place, you should always be open-minded about change, as these are plans about children who are growing and changing all the time – as are their circumstances, just like yours. A plan you've agreed upon should be committed to with all its rules and undertakings for a good innings, however. Reviews should be carried out at least every six months, and not just because a problem seems to have arisen. This is proactive parenting, and it helps you anticipate possible challenges and avert unnecessary complications. And your children will know their parents are getting together regularly to discuss them. With older children, you can involve them in family reviews where everybody can have their say, keeping in mind our advice in Chapter 4 about involving children in decision-making without abdicating parental care and authority.

> *'Don't ever say: "If it's okay with your father it's okay with me." This places an obligation on the child to check it out with the other parent, and if that parent decides it's NOT okay, then he (or she) is seen in a bad light. Check it out with him yourself if you think it's necessary, and then make your own decision. The kids can accept differences – it just means that Mum and Dad love them in different ways.'* EILEEN

Between you and your children

Many parents feel quite lost without touching base several times a day with their kids because they're used to feeling in touch, and this is the family's style. But shared parenting means you may have to review this. Think carefully, in this age of mobile phones and instant access, about what purpose keeping in touch all the time is really serving. Do you need to keep reassuring yourself, or making sure they're all right? Phone contact seems to quite often become a bone of contention, with parents accusing each other of discouraging phone calls between children and the parent they're not with. Children naturally tend to deal with their two-home situation by keeping them separate, and they may not benefit from too much overlap. Respecting the emotional boundaries that usefully exist between the households is important (see also Chapter 4). You are hoping to bring up emotionally independent children, after all. They aren't going to forget you while you're getting on with your life without them. If your relationship with your ex-partner and co-parent is often tense and hostile, and you have a parallel parenting arrangement, then we recommend minimum overlap between households.

'When I first heard about Mike's girlfriend, I was worried about how the children were going to feel. They said a few odd things about her that made me wonder what she was really like. But I managed to resist the temptation to talk about her too curiously. They soon seemed to take her for granted, and I guess it was just a matter of getting used to their dad moving on from me a step further.' AMY

Why are you calling?

Try asking yourself these questions, and your answers should help you pitch your contact right:
- Am I checking up on whether they're okay? Who is this going to help?
- Do I need to reassure myself they haven't forgotten me?
- Could they feel uncomfortable talking to me when they're over there? Will it help them if I insist?
- Am I afraid of them not needing me, of forgetting me?

> ■ If they seem to be calling me over an issue my ex
> should be dealing with, does it really help if I get
> involved? Might I unintentionally erode my ex's
> authority and competence?

Ideally, children should feel free to call sometimes with
exciting news, a goodnight message, or a homework problem
they know the other parent's good at, and they should be
encouraged by the parent they're with to feel free to do so.
But they shouldn't be calling because they've been made to
feel they must reassure this parent that they're okay, or if
they're worried that the parent is okay without them. If you
receive a call and you think your child is troubled, reassure
them in a way that transmits your confidence in their ability
to manage till you next see them, and encourage your ex-
partner to deal with these little uncertainties themselves.
Saying things at handovers like, 'Don't worry, I'll have the
phone on all the time if you need me' or 'If you're upset,
just call and I'll come and pick you up', or even 'I'll miss
you', tends to transmit uncertainty, and will contribute to
children's own anxieties. This is setting them up to feel
uncomfortable and insecure, and implying that the other
parent might not look after them properly. This is a burden
that they – and the other parent – just do not need.

> *'I thought it was really important for the kids to know
> I was thinking of them, so I always rang them to say
> goodnight.'* ALEX

Managing handovers

Communication at handover times is especially important, because changing from one parent to the other is often quite hard for children. If everything is going smoothly and you parents are friendly with one another, then lingering at handover is fine, sending a positive message about parental cooperation. If not, keep handovers brief. Cultivating your children's independence by having them run out to greet the other parent shows you're confident in them, and keeps uneasy parents apart. Even when there isn't tension between parents, it can be helpful for the children if you see them to school at the end of your 'shift' and have them go from school straight to their other home, even if some of their belongings have to go separately. This arrangement gives them six hours of emotionally neutral time as a kind of buffer between their two worlds, making the transition easier. Sometimes pick-ups and drop-offs can be done more smoothly through a third party such as a grandparent.

Michael says: Sometimes it helps, especially when you find it difficult or impossible to talk sensibly to your ex-partner, to look at your separation/divorce as a business. The nature of the business is parenting your children. The end products are healthy and happy children, growing into independent good citizens. The means of production are your parenting plan and the activities and attitudes that you put into it. You are both partners in the business of raising your children.

Jill says: Some parents worry about who should attend what school functions or whether both parents should always try to go. Both of you going and being together for them helps, but not if it generates tension that the children pick up. There may be sensitivities about new partners' involvement, too. Family occasions where you are together as a unit despite your separation shouldn't be avoided for fear of confusing the children. Such occasions show that you are still a family so far as their welfare and heritage are concerned. There's always a compromise possible!

Key messages

◆ Carefully plan difficult discussions with your ex-partner.

◆ It is crucial for co-parents to communicate constructively.

◆ It is important to commit to your parenting plan, but sometimes a review is necessary.

◆ Think of shared parenting as job-sharing.

◆ How you communicate can have different impacts.

◆ Don't contact your children excessively when they are with your ex.

◆ Handovers can be tricky.

Authors' notes

Page 4 'Research on the outcomes for children of divorce has produced varied results. However, there is agreement that separation poses serious risks for children in a number of ways...': Rodgers B & Prior J (1998) *Divorce and Separation: The outcomes for children,* Joseph Rowntree Foundation, York, England. Wallerstein J S, Lewis J M, Blakeslee S (2000), *The Unexpected Legacy of Divorce: The 25-year landmark study,* Hyperion, New York. Hetherington E N & Kelly J (2002) *For Better or Worse: Divorce reconsidered,* Norton & Co, New York.

Page 4 'Currently about 80 percent of children of separated families live in sole-mother custody arrangements, and as many as a third of them have little or no contact with their fathers...': Australian Bureau of Statistics (1998), *Family Characteristics Survey 1997,* Catalogue No 4442.0 ABS, Canberra. Office of National Statistics (UK), *Population Trends 1987.* Bradshaw J, Stimson C, Williams J and Skinner C (1999), *Absent Fathers,* London, Routledge. Trinder L, Beek M and Connolly J (2002), *Making Contact: How parents and children negotiate and experience contact after divorce,* YPS in association with Joseph Rowntree Foundation, USA.

Page 4 'The common arrangement for parenting children after divorce often leaves everyone dissatisfied ...': Fabricius W V & Hall J A (2000), 'Young adults' perspectives on divorce: living arrangements', *Family & Conciliation Courts Review*, 38: 446–461. Smart C, Neale B and Wade A (2001), *The Changing Experience of Childhood: Families and divorce*, Polity Press, Cambridge. Hunt J (2003), *Researching Contact*, London: National Council for One-Parent Families. Australian Institute of Family Studies, *Research Report No 9*, 2004, Bruce Smyth (ed). Laumann-Billings L and Emery R E (2000), 'Distress among young adults from divorced families', *Journal of Family Psychology*, 14: pp. 671–687. Blankenhorn D (1995), *Fatherless America: Confronting our most urgent social problem*, Basic Books, New York. Kruk E (1993), *Divorce and Disengagement: Patterns of fatherhood within and beyond marriage*, Fernwood Publications, Halifax NS. Greif G (1995), 'When divorced fathers want no contact with their children: a preliminary analysis', *Journal of Divorce and Remarriage*, 23: pp.75–84.

Page 4 'There is evidence that it does little for solid parent–child relationships, and can reduce one parent to onlooker status....': Laumann-Billings L & Emery R E (2000), 'Distress among young adults from divorced families', *Journal of Family Psychology*, 14:671–687. Ferro A (2004), ' "Standard" Contact in Parent–Child Contact and Post-Separation Arrangements', *AIFS Research Report No 9*. Hillery A, 'The Case for Joint Custody' in *The Best Parent is Both Parents,* David L Levy (ed) 1993, Hampton Roads Publishing, Norfolk VA. Roman M & Haddad W (1978), The Case for Joint Custody', *Psychology Today*, Sept: pp.196–205. Kelly J B (2005), 'Developing Beneficial Parenting Plan Models for Children Following Separation and Divorce', *Journal of the American Academy of Matrimonial Lawyers*, 19: pp.237–254.

Page 5 ' ... **children in shared care arrangements are more satisfied and appear to be better adjusted ...**': Kelly J (1988), 'Longer-term adjustment in children of divorce', *Journal of Family Psychology* 2 (2): pp.119–140. Bauserman R (2002), 'Child Adjustment in Joint Custody versus Sole-custody Arrangements: a meta-analytic review', *Journal of Family Psychology*, 16 (1): pp.91–102. Mosten J B, 'Dual household joint custody and adolescent separation-individuation', Dissertation for the Faculty of California Graduate Institute, July 2002.

Page 5 '**Because families are all so different, no one post-divorce arrangement can be said to be in the best interests of all children ...**': Lye D N (1999), *The Washington State Parenting Plan Study: Report to the Washington State Gender and Justice Commission and Domestic Relations Commission*, Washington Courts, Washington State. Mason M A (2000), *The Custody Wars*, Basic Books, New York. Ricci I, *Mom's House, Dad's House: Making two homes for your child*, Simon and Schuster, New York. Wallerstein J S and Blakeslee S (2003) *What About the Kids? Raising your children before, during and after divorce*, Hyperion, New York.

Page 6 '**Your children need time with both of their parents, time which is meaningful.**': Funder K (1996), *Remaking Families*, AIFS, Melbourne. Maccoby E E, Mnookin R H et. al. (1990), 'Private ordering revisited: what custodial arrangements are parents negotiating?' in D Sugarman and H H Kay (eds), *Divorce Reform at the Crossroads*, Yale UP. Wallerstein J and Blakeslee S (2003), *What About the Kids?* Hyperion Books, New York. Pryor J and Rogers B (2001), *Children in changing families: Life after parental separation*, Blackwell, Oxford. Smyth B, Caruana C and Ferro A (2003), 'Some whens, hows and whys of shared care: what separated parents who spend equal time with their children say about shared parenting', Australian Social Policy Conference, 2003.

Page 6 '**Shared parenting arrangements can produce happier children and more satisfied parents ...**': Parkinson P and Smyth B (2003), 'When the difference is night and day: some empirical insights into patterns of parent–child contact after separation', Paper presented at the 8th Australian Institute of Family Studies Conference, Melbourne. Smyth B, Sheehan G and Fehlberg B (2001), 'Patterns of Parenting After Divorce; a pre-Reform Act benchmark study', *Australian Journal of Family Law* 15(2) 114–128. Smyth B and Weston R (2004), 'Attitudes to 50/50 shared care in Australia', *Family Matters*, 63: pp.54–59. Oberg B & G (1985), *Den Delade Familjen*, Stockholm. Kelly J (1988), 'Longer-term adjustment in children of divorce', *Journal of Family Psychology* 2 (2): 119–140. Bauserman R (2002), 'Child adjustment in joint custody versus sole-custody arrangements: a meta-analytic review', *Journal of Family Psychology*, 16 (1): pp.91–102. Amato P R and Gilbreth J G (1999), 'Nonresidential fathers and children's well-being: a meta-analysis', *Journal of Marriage and the Family*, 61: pp.557–573. Dunn J (2003), 'Contact and children's perspectives on parental relationships', in A Bainham et. al. (eds), *Children and their Families: Contact, rights and welfare*, Hart Publishing, Oxford.

Page 14 '**Mediation, conflict-resolution programs and counselling have been shown to be successful in assisting separated parents to develop the attitudes and skills that enable them to become cooperative parents ...**': Kelly J B, 'Further Observations on Joint Custody', *University of California Davis Law Review*, Vol 16 p.762. Neff R & Cooper K (2004),

'Parental conflict resolution: Six-, Twelve- and Fifteen-Month Follow-ups of a High Conflict Program', *Family Court Review*, 42 (1): pp.99–114. McKenzie B & Guberman I (2000), 'For the Sake of the Children: a parent education program for separating and divorcing parents' (*Final Reports Phase 2*), Winnipeg: Faculty of Social Work, University of Manitoba. Bacon B L & McKenzie B (2004), 'Parent Education After Separation/Divorce: impact of the level of parental conflict on outcomes', *Family Court Review*, 42 (1): pp.85–98.

Page 16 '**There is reliable evidence that parents who have good relationships with their children pay more child support ...**': Australian Institute of Family Studies, Research Report No 9, 2004, Bruce Smyth (ed). Davis G and Wikely N (2002), 'National Survey of Child Support Agency Clients – the relationship dimension', *Family Law*, 32 (July): pp.522–527. Bradshaw J et. al. (1999), *Absent Fathers*, Routledge, London.

Page 20 '**All the research indicates that children hunger for the love and attention of their fathers, and are deeply affected when they don't get it.**': Stahl P M, 'A Review of Joint and Shared Parenting Literature', in Fohlberg J (ed) (*Joint Custody and Shared Parenting*, Washington DC Bureau of National Affairs, Association of Family & Conciliation Courts. Wallerstein J and Kelly J (1980), *Surviving the Break-up – how children and parents cope with divorce*, Grant McIntyre. Amato P R (2001), 'Children of divorce in the 1990s: an update of the Amato and Keith 1991 meta-analysis', *Journal of Family Psychology*, 15 (3): pp.355–370.

Page 20 '**If a father is discouraged from remaining or becoming involved, there are other consequences for mother, father and children.**': Stahl P M, 'A Review of Joint and Shared Parenting

Literature', in Fohlberg J (1984) (ed), *Joint Custody and Shared Parenting*, Washington DC Bureau of National Affairs, Association of Family & Conciliation Courts. Wallerstein J and Kelly J (1980), *Surviving the Break-up: How children and parents cope with divorce*, Grant McIntyre. Amato P R (2001), 'Children of divorce in the 1990s: an update of the Amato and Keith (1991) meta-analysis', *Journal of Family Psychology*, 15 (3): pp.355–370.

Page 22 '**Mothers with shared parenting may be less stressed and therefore better parents and workers ...**': Australian Institute of Family Studies, *Research Report No 9*, 2004, Bruce Smyth (ed).

Page 28 '**Research shows that the children who adjust best are the ones who don't lose a relationship with a parent because of a separation ...**': Pryor J and Rodgers B (2001), *Children in Changing Families: life after parental separation*, Blackwell Publishers, Oxford. Trinder L, Beek M and Connolly J (2002), *Making Contact: How parents and children negotiate and experience contact after divorce*, Joseph Rowntree Foundation, York. Arendell T (1996), *Co-parenting: a review of the literature*, National Center on Fathers and Families, Philadelphia. Benjamin M and Irving H H (1989), 'Shared Parenting: critical review of the research literature', *Family and Conciliation Courts Review*, 27 (2): pp.21–35. Australian Institute of Family Studies (2003), *Submission of the AIFS to the House of Representatives Standing Committee on Family and Community Affairs Inquiry into Child Custody Arrangements in the Event of Family Separation*, AIFS, Melbourne.

Page 29 '**It takes time, availability and repetition to make the bonding strong.**': Laumann-Billings L & Emery R E (2000), 'Distress among young adults from divorced families', *Journal of*

Family Psychology, 14: pp.671–687. Ferro A (2004), *'Standard'* *Contact in Parent–child Contact and Post-Separation Arrangements*, AIFS Research Report No 9.

Page 32 **'The stability that children need is more than geographical stability. It is *emotional stability* ...':** See Mosten J B, *Dual household joint custody and adolescent separation-individuation*, Dissertation for the Faculty of California Graduate Institute, July 2002. This is an important study. The author followed the attitudes and progress of 12 young people over two years, all of them in shared parenting situations. While disliking the hassles of living in two places, the young people were overwhelmingly in favour of shared custody, and could not imagine any alternative that would permit the same close relationship with both parents.

Page 36 **'There is growing evidence that overnight stays with important carers form a meaningful basis for parent–child relations from an early age.':** Pruett M K, Ebling R & Isabella G (2004), 'Critical Aspects of Parenting Plans for Young Children: injecting data into the debate about overnights', *Family Court Review*, 42 (1): pp.35–59. Warshak R (2000), 'Blanket Restrictions: overnight contact between parents and young children', *Family and Conciliation Courts Review*, 39 (4): pp.365–371. Kelly J B (2005), 'Developing Beneficial Parenting Plan Models for Children Following Separation and Divorce', *Journal of the American Academy of Matrimonial Lawyers*, 19: pp.237–254.

Page 38 **'Children need time to do ordinary things with each parent, not just fun things on holidays and weekends.':** Laumann-Billings L & Emery R E (2000), 'Distress among young adults from divorced families', *Journal of Family Psychology*, 14:

pp.671–687. Burgess A & Russell G (2003) in *Supporting Fathers: Contributions from the International Fatherhood Summit,* Oxford UK. See http://www.fathersdirect.com/index.php?id=12&cID=78.

Page 39 '**Authoritative and engaged parenting creates emotional bonding between father and child, which contributes significantly to the child's wellbeing ...**': Amato P R & Gilbreth J G (1999), 'Non-resident fathers and children's wellbeing: a meta-analysis', *Journal of Marriage and the Family,* 61: pp.557–573.

Page 40 '**This conclusion is inconsistent with research which show that good contact arrangements result in little conflict between parents.**': Smyth B, Caruana C & Ferro A (2004), 'Father–child contact after separation: profiling five different patterns of care', *Family Matters,* (67) Autumn. Pruett M K & Hoganbruen K (1998), 'Joint Custody and Shared Parenting, Research and Interventions', *Child and Adolescent Psychiatric Clinics of North America,* April, 7, No 2. Bauserman R (2002), 'Child Adjustment in Joint Custody versus Sole-custody Arrangements: a meta-analytic review', *Journal of Family Psychology,* 16 (1): pp.91–102.

Page 42 '**... children can cope with this as well as adults.**': Kelly J B (2000), 'Children's adjustment in conflicted marriage and divorce: a decade review of research', *Journal of American Academy of Child & Adolescent Psychiatry,* 39 (August): p.8.

Page 47 '**So, care needs to be taken in involving children in separation planning ...**': Smart C (2002), 'From Children's Shoes to Children's Voices', *Family Court Review,* 40 (3): pp.307–319.

Kaltenborn K (2004), 'Parent–child Contact after Divorce: the need to consider the child's perspective', *Marriage and Family Review*, 36 (1): pp.67–90.

Page 48 '**A mother and father with different parenting styles can complement one another effectively.**': Pruett M K, (2000), *Fatherneed: Why father care is as essential as mothercare for your child,* The Free Press, New York.

Page 51 '**Litigation exacerbates conflict between parents and increases pressure on children.**': Zaidel S (2004), 'Taking Divorce out of the Context of Dispute Resolution', *Family Court Review*, 42 (4): pp.678–680. Ricci I (1997), *Mom's House, Dad's House: Making two homes for your children,* Simon & Schuster, New York. Luepnitz D A (1982), *Child Custody: A study of families after divorce,* Lexington MA, Lexington Books.

Page 51 '**Children pick up on continuing parental conflict and it can have seriously damaging consequences for them …**': Amato P R & Gilbreth J G (1999), 'Non-resident fathers and children's well-being: a meta-analysis', *Journal of Marriage and the Family,* 61: pp.557–573. Bauserman (2002), 'Child Adjustment in Joint-Custody versus Sole-Custody Arrangements: a meta-analytic review', *Journal of Family Psychology*, 16 (1): pp.91–102. Lee M-Y (2002), 'A model of children's post-divorce behavioural adjustment in maternal and dual residence arrangements', *Journal of Family Issues*, 23 (5): pp.672–697. Pryor J and Daly-Peoples R (2001), 'Adolescent attitudes toward living arrangements after divorce', *Child and Family Law Quarterly*, 13 (2): pp.197–208. Amato P R and Rezac S J (1994), 'Contact with nonresidential parents, interparental conflict, and children's behaviour', *Journal of Family Issues*, 15 (2): pp.191–207. Reynolds J (ed) (2001), *Not in Front* *of the Children? How conflict between parents affects children,* One Plus One Marriage and Partnership Research, London.

Page 53 '**Divorce can be a trigger for improved relationships between children and parents, especially for fathers ...**': Wallerstein J & Kelly J B (1980), *Surviving the Break-up: How children and parents cope with divorce,* Grant McIntyre. Smyth B, Caruana C and Ferro A (2003), 'Some whens, hows and whys of shared care: what separated parents who spend equal time with their children say about shared parenting', Paper presented at the Australian Social Policy Conference, Sydney, July.

Page 59 '**As we noted in Chapter 2, recent research into shared parenting suggests that it works for kids if it's managed in a child-focused way, but not if it's managed in a competitive, adult-focused way.**': Neale B, Flowerdew J & Smart C (2003), 'Drifting Towards Shared Residence? Report from Centre for Research on Family, Kinship and Childhood (Leeds)', *Family Law,* December 2003, 904–908. Irving H H and Benjamin M (1989), 'Shared Parenting: critical review of the research literature', *Family and Conciliation Courts Review,* 27 (2): pp.21–35.

Page 78 '**... there are good reasons why care needs to be taken here...**': Smart C (2002), 'From Children's Shoes to Children's Voices', *Family Court Review,* 40 (3): pp.307–319. Kaltenborn K (2004), 'Parent–child Contact after Divorce: the need to consider the child's perspective', *Marriage and Family Review,* 36 (1): pp.67–90.

Page 82 '**US experience suggests that children, as well as adults, benefit from programs that help them cope with the changes in their lives due to their parents' separation**': Pedro-Carroll J L

(2005), 'Fostering Resilience in the Aftermath of Divorce: The Role of Evidence-Based Programs for Children', *Family Court Review*, 43 (1): pp.52–64. Wolchik, S A et. al. (2005), 'Programs for Promoting Parenting of Residential Parents: moving from efficacy to effectiveness', *Family Court Review*, 43 (1): pp.65–80.

Page 93 '**Even very young children can benefit from overnight stays with another parent...**': Kelly J B & Lamb M E (2000), 'Using child development research to make appropriate custody and access decisions for young children', *Family and Conciliation Courts Review*, 38: pp.297–311. Lamb M E & Kelly J B (2001), 'Using the empirical literature to guide the development of parenting plans for young children', *Family Court Review*, 39 (4) pp.365–371. Warshak R (2000), 'Blanket restrictions: overnight contact between parents and young children', *Family and Conciliation Courts Review*, 38: pp.422–445.

Page 106 '**For parents who find it impossible to get along, 'parallel parenting' can work...**': Parallel parenting plans can work for children of estranged parents. Richard Warshak, author of *Divorce Poison: Protecting the Parent–child Bond from a Vindictive Ex*, estimates that more than half of divorced parents sharing custody in the US follow this path. See also Smyth B, Caruana C & Ferro A (2004), 'Father–child Contact after Separation: profiling five different patterns of care', *Family Matters*, 67 (Autumn). Ricci I (1997), *Mom's House, Dad's House: Making two homes for your children*, Simon & Schuster, New York. Furstenberg F F Jr and Cherlin A J (1991), *Divided Families: What happens to children when parents part*, Harvard University Press, Cambridge, Mass.

Acknowledgements

The authors send warm thanks and appreciation to the many mothers, fathers, sons and daughters who were willing to share their experiences of life after divorce and separation. Through their generosity, this book rests securely on real life as well as on academic research.

Helpful resources

Most people need help through and in the aftermath of separation and divorce. Our experience is that this help is found with good divorce counsellors, quality mediators, and sensible lawyers.

We also recommend post-separation parenting courses. There is overwhelming evidence that intensive programs – as opposed to information sessions – can change both attitudes and behaviour, and lead to better parenting of children in separated families.

Such programs can be accessed through the family courts, community welfare organisations and separation counsellors. Many can be found on the Internet.

Recommended reading

Constance R Ahrons, *The Good Divorce,* Bloomsbury, New York, 1995

Maurice Balson, *Becoming Better Parents,* Australian Council for Educational Research, Melbourne, 1991

Steve Biddulph, *Raising Boys,* 2nd edition, Finch Publishing, Sydney, 2003

Steve Biddulph, *The Secret of Happy Children,* Harper Collins, Sydney, 1994

Robert Brooks and Sam Goldstein, *Raising Resilient Children: Fostering strength, hope and optimism in your child,* Contemporary Books, McGraw-Hill, New York, 2001

Jill Burrett, *Dad's Place: A new guide for fathers after divorce,* Carrington Psychology, Sydney, 2001

Jill Burrett, *Parenting After Separation: Making the most of family changes,* Finch Publishing, Sydney, 2002

Robert E Emery, *The Truth about Children and Divorce: Dealing with the emotions so you and your children can thrive,* Penguin, New York, 2004

Miriam Galper, *Co-Parenting: Sharing your children equally*, AFCC Publications, Madison, USA. See also http://www.afccnet.org/resources/resources_parents.asp

Dr Thomas Gordon, *Parent Effectiveness Training*, Three Rivers Press, New York, 2000

John Gottman, *The Heart of Parenting: How to raise an emotionally intelligent child*, Bloomsbury, London, 1997

Dr Christopher Green, *Beyond Toddlerdom: Keeping five- to twelve-year-olds on the rails*, Doubleday, Sydney, 2000

Planning for Shared Parenting: A Guide for Parents Living Apart, AFCC Publications, Madison, USA

Isolina Ricci, *Mom's House, Dad's House: A complete guide for parents who are separated, divorced or remarried*, AFCC Publications, Madison, USA, 1997

Matthew R Sanders, *Every Parent: A positive approach to children's behaviour*, Penguin, Melbourne, 2004

Other Finch titles of interest

By the same author

Parenting after Separation
Making the most of family changes
Jill Burrett
So much parenting now takes place from two households, following separation. This book offers positive approaches to caring for children and dealing with your new and complex roles.
ISBN 1876451 378

Adolescence
A guide for parents
In this informative and wide-ranging book, Michael Carr-Gregg and Erin Shale help parents understand what is happening for young people aged 10–20 and how to deal with it. They discuss the big questions in a young person's life and provide parents and teachers with useful approaches for handling problems. ISBN 1876451 351

Bouncing Back
How to overcome setbacks, become resilient and create a happier life
This practical book outlines some approaches to cope with the initial trauma of loss and failure – and to find ways to recover. Brian Babington's approaches will help people who have experienced severe loss – such as a death in the family – or other traumatic events, such as the breakdown of a relationship or the loss of a job. ISBN 1876451 564

Chasing Ideas
The fun of freeing your child's imagination
Christine Durham teaches thinking skills to children, and in this book she encourages parents and teachers to see how discussing ideas with their children (aged 4 to 14) can be an enjoyable and creative activity for everyone.
ISBN 1876451 181

Confident Parenting
How to set limits, be considerate and stay in charge
Dr William Doherty
'We may be the most child-sensitive generations of parents the world has ever known – and the most confused and insecure,' says the author. This book shows you how to parent effectively and how to ensure that your family is not overwhelmed by external pressures such as advertising, TV and peer culture.
ISBN 1876451 467

Dealing with Anger
Self-help solutions for men
Frank Donovan
Focussing on emotional healing and practical change, this book includes case studies from clients of the author's (a psychotherapist) and a program of exercises for the reader.
ISBN 1876451 05X

Father and Child Reunion
How to bring the dads we need to the children we love
Dr Warren Farrell
This book calls for a rejoining of families (and of children with parents who can care for them) by creating equal opportunities for men as parents. ISBN 1876451 327

Fathering from the Fast Lane
Practical ideas for busy dads
Dr Bruce Robinson
The pressures of working life today mean that many fathers are not spending the time with their children that they would like. This book

presents practical and straightforward ways to improve this situation. In this collection of valuable fathering ideas, over 75 men from various backgrounds speak about how they balance demanding jobs with being a good dad. ISBN 1876451 211

Getting on With Others
How to teach your child essential social skills
John Cooper
Cooperative children do better at school and in life; they learn how to make friends, manage their emotions and solve problems with others. John Cooper, who has 30 years of clinical practice working with children and families, shows how parents can teach these skills to children from 3 to 7. ISBN 1876451 696

The Happiness Handbook
Strategies for a happy life
Dr Timothy Sharp
'Happiness is no more than a few simple disciplines practiced every day; while misery is simply a few errors in judgement repeated every day.' So says Dr Sharp, founder of the Happiness Institute in Australia and author of this innovative and inspiring book. ISBN 1876451 645

Kids Food Health
Nutrition and your child's development
The authors, Dr Patricia McVeagh – a paediatrician – and Eve Reed – a dietitian – present the parents of children from newborns to teenagers with the latest information on the impact of diet on health, growth, allergies, behaviour and physical development.
Kids Food Health 1: *The first year*
ISBN 1876451 149
Kids Food Health 2: *From toddler to preschooler* ISBN 1876451 157
Kids Food Health 3: *From school-age to teenage* ISBN 1876451 165

Manhood
An action plan for changing men's lives
(3rd edition)
Steve Biddulph tackles the key areas of a man's life – parenting, love and sexuality, finding meaning in work, and making real friends. He presents new pathways to healing the past and forming true partnerships with women, as well as honouring our own inner needs. ISBN 1876451 203

Men After Separation
Surviving and growing when your relationship ends
Ian Macdonald
'Men often react disastrously to a marriage ending. This book gives a frank and direct approach to men's practical concerns, emotional needs, sexuality, and the importance of clear and rational thinking. Highly recommended.' *Steve Biddulph*
ISBN 1876451610

On Their Own
Boys growing up underfathered
Rex McCann
For a young man, growing up without an involved father in his life can leave a powerful sense of loss. *On Their Own* considers the needs of young men as they mature, the passage from boyhood to manhood, and the roles of fathers and mothers. ISBN 1876451 084

Parenting for Character
Equipping your child for life
Andrew Mullins
A practical guide to assist parents in encouraging their children to think independently, to develop habits that lead to good character, and to make choices that are good for themselves and others. ISBN 1876451 661

Raising Boys
Why boys are different – and how to help them become happy and well-balanced men (2nd edn)
In this international bestseller, Steve Biddulph examines the crucial ways that boys differ from girls. He looks at boys' development from birth to manhood and discusses the warm, strong parenting and guidance boys need.
ISBN 1876451 505 *Also:*
Raising Boys Audio: A double-cassette set read by Steve Biddulph. ISBN 1876451 254

Raising Girls
Why girls are different – and how to help them grow up happy and strong
Gisela Preuschoff injects her own experiences as a mother of four into this book, and illustrates her points with stories and examples from the experiences of many families. Her advice ranges from birth to late adolescence – and across physical and sexual development, schools and learning, gender stereotyping, parent–child relationships and a girl's emotional life. ISBN 1876451 599

Starting School
How to help your child be prepared
Sue Berne
How a child starts off at school plays an important role in determining their approach to education throughout life. This book will help you ensure that your child's practical, emotional and social skills are sufficiently developed to make the most of starting school.
ISBN 1876451 475

Stepfamily Life
Why it is different – and how to make it work
In Margaret Newman's experience, stepfamily life *is* different, and therefore different solutions are needed to get it 'on track' – and, more importantly, to help it survive. Margaret considers a wide range of stepfamily scenarios, and gives practical suggestions about what to do in each case to overcome any difficulties.
ISBN 1876451 521

Take Control of Your Life
The five-step plan to health and happiness
(2nd edition)
Dr Gail Ratcliffe
This book is a blueprint for recognising what is wrong with your life, minimising your stress, and maximising the opportunities to reach your goals. The author, a clinical psychologist, has developed her five-step method of life-planning and stress management with clients for over 13 years. ISBN 1876451 513

Teen Stages
How to guide the journey to adulthood
Ken & Elizabeth Mellor
One of the Mellors' key concepts is that teenagers grow through six very distinct developmental stages, each requiring specific responses that rarely work for the others. To help parents and teachers, the Mellors offer numerous practical, tested suggestions and give many simple hints on how to head off 'trouble' before it starts. ISBN 1876451 386

Your Child's Emotional Needs
What they are and how to meet them
Dr Vicky Flory
This unique book explains the connections between children's emotions and their behaviour, overall wellbeing, friendships, school performance and their ability to adjust to adolescence. (Ages 0–12)
ISBN 1876451 653

For further information on our titles, visit our website: www.finch.com.au

Index